T0328231

London
Hidden Walks

Pete Smith

Published by Geographers'
A-Z Map Company Limited
An imprint of HarperCollins Publishers
Westerhill Road
Bishopbriggs
Glasgow
G64 2QT

HarperCollins*Publishers*
Macken House, 39/40 Mayor Street Upper
Dublin 1, D01 C9W8, Ireland

www.az.co.uk
a-z.maps@harpercollins.co.uk

1st edition 2022

Text and routes © Pete Smith 2022
Mapping © Collins Bartholomew Ltd 2022

This product uses map data licenced from
Ordnance Survey© Crown copyright and
database rights 2021 OS 100018598

AZ, A-Z and AtoZ are registered trademarks
of Geographers' A-Z Map Company Limited

All rights reserved. No part of this publication may be
reproduced, stored in a retrieval system, or transmitted,
in any form or by any means, electronic, mechanical,
photocopying, recording or otherwise without the prior
permission in writing of the publisher and copyright owners.

Every care has been taken in the preparation of this atlas.
However, the Publisher accepts no responsibility whatsover
for any loss, damage, injury or inconvenience sustained
or caused as a result of using this atlas. The representation
of a road, track or footpath is no evidence of a right of way.

A catalogue record for this book
is available from the British Library.

ISBN 978-0-00-849634-0

10 9 8 7 6 5 4

Printed in India

MIX
Paper | Supporting
responsible forestry
FSC™ C007454

This book is produced from independently certified FSC™ paper
to ensure responsible forest management.

For more information visit: www.harpercollins.co.uk/green

contents

introduction

From its foundation by the Romans two thousand years ago, London has grown into a truly global city, with a population of over nine million people speaking more than three hundred languages. Its worldwide reputation as a centre for culture, entertainment and the arts, together with its string of iconic buildings and fine stores, make it a must-see destination, and in 2015 it was the most visited city in the world, attracting sixty-five million tourists.

But London has more to offer the explorer than its museums, its great parks, its theatres and concert venues, and such world-famous tourist magnets as Buckingham Palace and St Paul's Cathedral. It is a busy, vibrant, living city, full of diversity, contrasts and oddities. Indeed, many Londoners see their city as a collection of villages, each with its own distinctive character.

The twenty walking tours in this collection, each supported by detailed A-Z mapping, take in many of the established gems of the capital, from Tower Bridge to the Houses of Parliament and from Greenwich to Trafalgar Square. They also set out, though, to explore the individual characteristics of some of the capital's 'villages' and to pinpoint a few of the intriguing little secrets and eccentricities that any great city accumulates over the years. Readers can expect to encounter, among other curiosities, a memorial to mice, a former police station housed in a pillar, a hat-eating wombat, a fine-dining wooden cat, two cherubs making a telephone call, and a drunken elephant.

about the author

A Cambridge English graduate with a lifelong interest in London, Pete Smith is married with two children and three grandchildren. After a career as a university teacher, he retrained as a London guide, and is currently a freelance lecturer and tourist guide with his own small walking tour company, London City Walks.

how to use this book

Each of the 20 walks in this guide is set out in a similar way. They are all introduced with a brief description, including notes on things you will encounter on your walk, and a photograph of a place of interest you might pass along the way.

On the first page of each walk there is a panel of information outlining the distance of the walk, a guide to the walking time, and a brief description of the path conditions

or the terrain you will encounter. A suggested starting point along with the nearest postcode is shown, although postcodes can cover a large area therefore this is just a rough guide.

The major part of each section is taken up with route maps and detailed point-to-point directions for the walk. The route instructions are prefixed by a number in a circle, and the corresponding location is shown on the map.

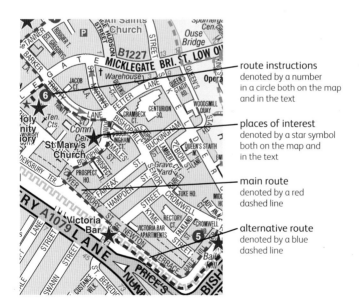

route instructions
denoted by a number
in a circle both on the map
and in the text

places of interest
denoted by a star symbol
both on the map and
in the text

main route
denoted by a red
dashed line

alternative route
denoted by a blue
dashed line

AZ walk one

The City's Bridges: North Bank

Blackfriars to the Tower.

In the year 43, Roman invaders established a base camp at a bridgeable point on the tidal River Thames, and London was born. For nearly 2,000 years this area, the Pool of London, was a teeming world port, and from the very beginning there was a bridge, or rather a succession of wooden bridges, spanning the river, until in 1176 work began on a stone bridge. This bridge was built under the supervision of a priest, Peter de Colechurch, who died before it was completed and was buried in a chapel in the middle of his bridge. Tolls were charged and gifts were made 'to God and the Bridge' to fund repairs, and in 1282 the Bridge House Trust was founded to maintain London Bridge.

Today there are five bridges over the Thames in the City of London, and the City Bridge Trust is responsible for the upkeep of all of them: Tower (technically some yards outside the Square Mile of the City), London, Southwark, Millennium and Blackfriars.

This walk explores the City's historic waterfront and the bridges that span the river along it, and can be combined with walk 4 to create a circular walk returning along the south bank.

start	Blackfriars Underground Station (Circle and District lines)
nearest postcode	EC4V 4DD
finish	Tower Hill Underground Station (Circle and District lines)
distance	1¾ miles / 2.7 km (4 miles / 6.4 km if combined with walk 4)
time	1 hour (2¼ hours if combined with walk 4)
terrain	Surfaced roads and paths; steps to climb and descend; no steep hills.

1 From Blackfriars Station ★ , go left onto the bridge ★ and take the steps down to St Paul's Walk. Head east under the Millennium Bridge ★ . The first Thames pedestrian crossing in a hundred years, this opened in June 2000 to link St Paul's Cathedral to Tate Modern on the south bank but soon became notorious as 'the wobbly bridge' and was closed until February 2002 while modifications were made. It cost £18,000,000 to build and a further £5,000,000 to stabilize.

2 Continue to Broken Wharf. Turn left inland and right along High Timber Street before rejoining the river walkway at Queenhithe, where a mosaic traces the course of the Thames to the sea and touches on some milestones of London history. Queenhithe, one of hundreds of small moorings along the river frontage, was once the most important dock in London. The 12th-century queen in question was Matilda, who built London's first post-Roman public lavatory nearby.

3 Turn left past the plaque to Alfred the Great, and enter Fruiterers' Passage under Vintners' Hall and Southwark Bridge ★ . The wall panels suggest how this area once looked.

4 Leaving Fruiterers' Passage, continue to Walbrook Walk where the River Walbrook used to enter the Thames. The Waste Transfer Station here sends the City's waste by barge to an incineration plant downriver. Appropriately, Dick Whittington sited a public lavatory here twice as large as Queen Matilda's: a 128-seater flushed twice a day by the tide!

5 Passing The Banker pub, take Steelyard Passage under Cannon Street Station. An art installation recalls the course of the river through floor-level lighting and plays riverside sounds. The Steelyard was occupied for 400 years by a guild of Hanseatic traders expelled by Elizabeth I in the late 1500s.

6 Ahead, beyond Fishmongers' Hall, the present London Bridge ★ was finished in 1972. Its predecessor was re-erected in Lake Havasu City, Arizona. Notice the multiple sets of mooring rings on the arch; there is a difference of as much as 26 feet (8 metres) between high and low tides here.

7 After you have passed under London Bridge, stop to look at the view of The Shard ★ on the south side of the river. At 1,017 feet (310 metres), it is the tallest building in Western Europe. Its designer, Renzo Piano, claimed it was inspired by the spires of the churches in London designed by Christopher Wren. The gardens on your left lead to the church of St Magnus the Martyr. The eastern footway of Old London Bridge once passed through the tower, and the church contains a model of the old bridge. On the far bank, between London and Tower Bridges, was Hay's Wharf, the oldest and largest wharf in the Port of London.

8 Billingsgate Market ★ ahead used to be famous for fish and bad language. The fish market moved to Tower Hamlets in 1982, but Horace Jones's 1877 chateau-like market buildings remain. Jones was also partly responsible for Tower Bridge ★ downriver. Look for the fish figures on top of the street lamps in front of the market building. Next, you will pass the Georgian Custom House ★ , which in its heyday accommodated 2,000 customs officials.

9 Keep following the riverside path as far as the Tower of London ★ . If you wish to combine this walk with walk 4, continue past the Tower and under the bridge to join the walk at step 2. To conclude the walk here, turn left up Tower Hill, cross the road at the traffic lights, and go diagonally right across Trinity Square Gardens to Tower Hill Underground Station ★ .

AZ walk two

Seething, Mincing and Staining

The historic lanes and alleys of the Square Mile.

Despite the Great Fire of 1666, the damage caused by two world wars, and centuries of redevelopment, much of the City's medieval street plan of narrow, winding lanes and alleys remains.

This walk links three iconic sites, the Tower of London, Guildhall and St Paul's Cathedral, but most of the route leads through the workaday world of a lively community built on trade and worship. Before 1666 there were 109 churches within the Square Mile, and in many parishes most residents followed the same occupation. Frequently, religious fraternities that were set up in individual churches became trade guilds, which in turn developed into livery companies with royal charters entitling them to a coat of arms and a distinctive livery or uniform. Throughout the walk there are reminders of the lives, work and worship of long-gone Londoners, not just in the often strange names of the thoroughfares but also in the churches and livery halls along the way.

start	Tower Hill Underground Station (Circle and District lines)
nearest postcode	EC3N 1JL
finish	St Paul's Station (Central Line)
distance	2 miles / 3.4 km
time	1½ hours
terrain	Surfaced roads and paths; steps to climb and descend; no steep hills.

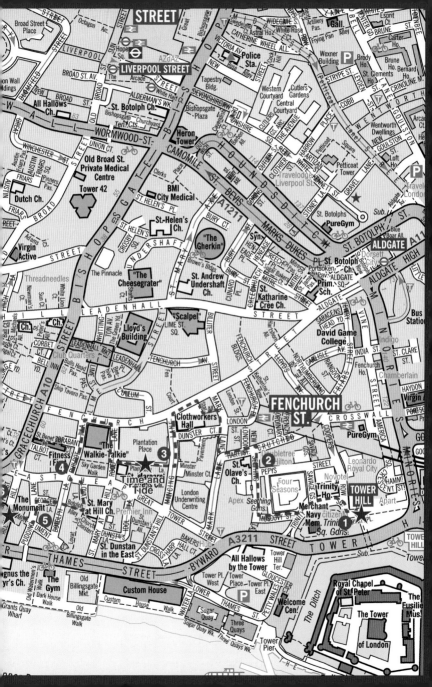

❶ The walk begins at Tower Hill Underground Station ★ . Leaving the station, turn right up Coopers Row and cross left into Trinity Square. Pass Trinity House and the old Port of London Authority building to enter Muscovy Street and bear right into Seething Lane, once home to the Navy Office and its senior staff, including Samuel Pepys. Corn used to be threshed in this area, and 'seething' refers to the clouds of chaff this raised.

❷ Continue past the macabre gateway to St Olave's churchyard to the T junction with Crutched Friars, named after the Friars of the Holy Cross, the Fratres Cruciferi, or 'Crutched Friars'. Turn left along Hart Street, cross Mark (originally Mart or Market) Lane, and go right. Passing the tower of All Hallows Staining (the stone church), turn left into Star Alley. In Fenchurch Street, turn left and left again into Mincing Lane; the 'mynchen' or nuns of St Helen's Bishopsgate owned property here.

❸ Cross over at Plantation Lane on the right to see the 'Time and Tide' ★ art installation on the ground. Follow the lane ahead to Rood Lane where a huge cross or 'rood' once stood. Cross Rood Lane, turn right and at Fenchurch Street turn left and left again. At the foot of Philpot Lane, look up to see two red mice nibbling a piece of yellow cheese. In the 1800s, a plasterer working on the building accused his workmate of eating his sandwiches. They fought, and one man fell to his death. The real culprits were mice!

❹ Go left along Eastcheap, and use the traffic island to cross to Lovat Lane (formerly Love Lane). Turn right into Botolph Alley, and cross Botolph Lane into St George's Lane, leading into Pudding Lane. Go left down Pudding Lane to where a plaque commemorates the starting point of the Great Fire. Eastcheap up the hill was a street of butchers' shops, and the 'puddings' were offal carted down to the river.

❺ Cross the square to The Monument ★ , which celebrates London's recovery after the fire and stands on the site of the first church that it claimed. Close to Monument Underground Station and several pubs and other eating places, this is a good point for a break.

❻ From The Monument, take Monument Street, turn right and at the traffic lights cross King William Street to go left along Cannon Street and left down Martin Lane. By The Old Wine Shades pub, turn right and cross Laurence Pountney Lane. Past the churchyard of St Laurence Pountney, go right up Pountney Hill.

7 Reaching Cannon Street (originally the street of candlemakers), turn left. Just past Cannon Street Station, cross the road and turn left down Dowgate Hill, crossing Cloak Lane. Four livery companies have their halls in Dowgate Hill: the Tallow Chandlers, the Skinners, the Dyers and the Innholders. Just before Innholders' Hall, turn right into College Street. Dick Whittington, who was Lord Mayor of London in the late 14th and early 15th centuries, founded the College of St Spirit and St Mary in the church of St Michael Paternoster ★ , lived around the corner and is buried in the church.

8 Continue through Skinners Lane to the church of St James Garlickhithe, named after a wharf where garlic and spices were unloaded. Turn right and walk up Garlick Hill to Mansion House Station, where you can cross by subway to walk up Bow Lane.

9 At Cheapside, cross by the traffic island to Honey Lane. Cheapside was once the City's main shopping street (the Anglo-Saxon word 'ceap' meant to sell or to barter), and each commodity had its own area. Turn right at the end of Honey Lane to reach King Street, turn left to cross Trump Street and walk up to Gresham Street.

10 Cross at the traffic lights towards the 15th-century Guildhall ★ , still the administrative centre of the City. In Guildhall Yard, go left past the church of St Lawrence Jewry (this area housed the Jewish financiers brought from Normandy by William the Conqueror), and skirt the pond to enter Aldermanbury. Go right as far as Love Lane, and cross left to continue past City of London Police Headquarters. Ahead, on the other side of Wood Lane, pass through At Alban's Court then go left down Staining Lane. Recorded as Stayning Lane in the 16th century, this street name is named for the people of Staines in Middlesex. Cross Gresham Street into Gutter Lane, where a family called Gutherun lived a thousand years ago.

11 Where Gutter Lane meets Cheapside, turn right towards St Paul's Cathedral. Just past Foster Lane, cross at the traffic lights to St Paul's Underground Station where the walk ends.

AZ walk three

The Heart of the City

High finance and high buildings.

This circular walk takes in five fine churches, the financial centre of the Square Mile and some exciting modern architecture. Along the way, it includes part of the Roman fort and a temple dedicated to the god Mithras.

From the late 1200s, London's banking clustered around Lombard Street. The neighbouring Royal Exchange was opened as a trading centre in the 1500s by Sir Thomas Gresham, and in 1694 the Bank of England was established nearby. Coffee houses appeared in the 1650s and became meeting places for businessmen (Lloyd's insurance company began in a coffee house). Banks proliferated in the 1800s, and the frieze on the National Provincial Bank building gives a realistic sense of where the nation's wealth then came from.

From the 1960s, the City began building high, and this route includes the tallest City tower, the Pinnacle, as well as earlier contenders: Tower 42, Heron Tower and the once controversial but now iconic Gherkin. Londoners love nicknaming their skyscrapers, and you will also catch glimpses of The Cheesegrater and The Scalpel.

start / finish	Mansion House Underground Station (Circle and District lines)
nearest postcode	EC4M 9BW
distance	3 miles / 5 km
time	1 hour 45 minutes
terrain	Surfaced roads and paths; steps to climb; one medium steep hill.

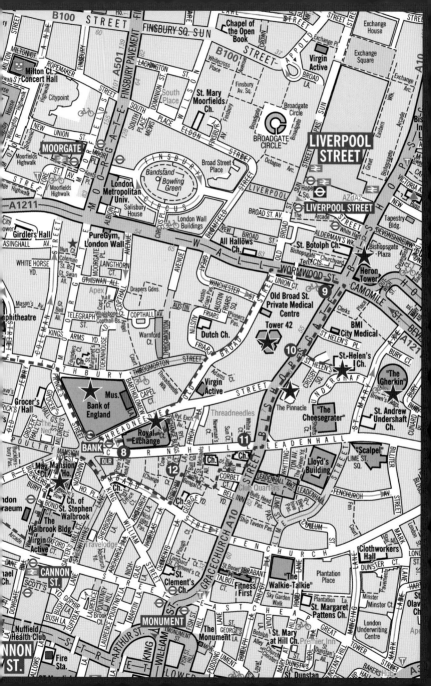

1 Take the Bow Lane exit from Mansion House Station. Pass St Mary Aldermary Church, with its breathtaking fan-vaulted ceiling, on your right, go on to cross Watling Street, and turn left into Bow Churchyard. Every true Londoner must be born within the sound of Bow Bells. Cross the churchyard and go through the passage opposite the church.

2 In Bread Street, turn right and then left along Cheapside's shopping mall, One New Change. Halfway along the building, go through the entrance on the left, and take the central lift ahead to Floor 6. The terrace here gives a spectacular view of St Paul's Cathedral ★ and the surrounding skyline.

3 After this, take the lift down to street level and leave the complex towards St Paul's. Go left along New Change, cross to the right at the traffic lights, and continue along Cannon Street into St Paul's Churchyard. When you see across the road the open space leading to the Millennium Bridge, cross at the lights to look back at the cathedral. In the triangular pediment below the dome is the figure of a phoenix rising from its own ashes and Christopher Wren's motto for St Paul's, 'Resurgam' (I shall rise again). The cathedral was destroyed in the 1666 Great Fire, rebuilt by Wren and threatened again by fire in the Second World War.

4 Turning left towards the bridge, walk to the Firefighters Memorial and go right, behind the Information Centre and across Godliman Street, into Carter Lane, once an important City thoroughfare. Pass the Youth Hostel and Wardrobe Place: for centuries the King's Wardrobe storing thousands of items stood here.

5 Go left down St Andrew's Hill as far as the Cockpit pub. After King Henry VIII shut down Blackfriars Monastery in 1538, Shakespeare bought the gatehouse on this site as a buy-to-let. Turn right through Ireland Yard and Playhouse Yard, and right again up Black Friars Lane, past Apothecaries' Hall. Continuing along Ludgate Broadway, look left down Pilgrim Street for a view of St Bride's Church with its wedding-cake spire, before going right, up Ludgate Hill, towards St Paul's.

6 Cross at the pedestrian crossing to face the cathedral by the statue to Queen Anne (noticing the figure of America with her foot on the head of a decapitated European!). Continue along the left side of the cathedral to the junction of New Change and Paternoster Row, where you go left to the lights and cross Cheapside to the right side of St Martin's Le Grand. Cross Gresham Street, bear right at the Museum of London down London Wall and take the first right down Noble Street.

7 Continue past the remains of the City Wall and a Roman watchtower to Gresham Street, where you turn left opposite Goldsmiths' Hall. Past the entrance to Guildhall Yard, cross at the traffic lights and keep on along Gresham Street to cross Princes Street. Turning right along the eight-feet-thick wall of the Bank of England ★, continue to Bank Junction, where you cross Threadneedle Street at the traffic lights to the space outside the Royal Exchange ★. Here, you can look back to the Mansion House ★, the Lord Mayor's official residence, across to the Bank of England (whose vaults are as deep as the Bank is tall), and ahead to the Royal Exchange.

8 Go through the Exchange building, now a luxurious centre for eating, drinking and shopping, and at the far end turn left along Royal Exchange Buildings. At Threadneedle Street, cross to the right side of Old Broad Street and walk past the base of Tower 42 (formerly the NatWest Tower) ★. At the T junction, turn right towards Bishopsgate. Across and on your left is Heron Tower ★, and to your right is The Pinnacle ★.

9 Cross Bishopsgate and go right. Opposite Tower 42, take the left-hand turning into the churchyard of St Helen Bishopsgate ★, which is known for its many monuments. The right doorway is that of the original parish church; the one to its left was once the entrance to a Benedictine nunnery. Behind the church is The Gherkin ★.

10 Returning to Bishopsgate, turn left. Across the street is the former National Provincial Bank. Continue, to cross first Leadenhall Street ahead and then Gracechurch Street to the right.

11 Turn left and then right into the narrow St Peter's Alley. At The Counting House pub (Scrooge's office in Charles Dickens' *A Christmas Carol* was set close by), go left to face the side of another pub. On your left, set into the wall, is the oldest livery company mark in the City, the demi-virgin of the Mercers' Company, showing their ownership of this site. Go up the steps on your right and bear right behind St Michael's Church to the Jamaica Wine House. Here was the site of London's first coffee house. Turn left past The George & Vulture pub and sharp right into Bengal Court.

12 At Birchin Lane, turn left and then go right along Lombard Street, turning right at the T junction. By Bank Station entrance, cross the road and turn left past the front of the Mansion House into Walbrook. Passing the Church of St Stephen Walbrook (Christopher Wren's first domed church) and the Roman Mithraeum, turn right through Bloomberg's European HQ along Watling Street, a Roman and Saxon thoroughfare. Crossing at the traffic lights on your left, continue along the side of St Mary Aldermary and turn left down Bow Lane to return to Mansion House Station.

A̅Z̅ walk four

The City's Bridges: South Bank

The Tower to Blackfriars.

Starting from Tower Bridge, the route follows the south bank of the river and provides spectacular views of the City as we walk towards London Bridge. The first stone bridge here lasted for nearly 600 years until 1832. Its nineteen piers obstructed the river, producing rapids between them around high and low tide while creating a millpond effect upriver. Under the next bridge, Southwark, tiled reproductions of popular engravings recall the Frost Fairs that took place on this stretch of the River Thames until 1814. The ice was thick enough even for oxen to be roasted on it, and at the last such fair an elephant was walked across the river.

The Millennium Bridge comes next and is followed by Blackfriars. Railway companies raced to bring their tracks into the City, and the walk also features two railway bridges (not maintained by the City). There are, though, no traces of the hundreds of ferrymen who lost their livelihoods as new bridges arrived.

If you start this walk by midday on a Monday to Saturday, you will be able to catch Borough Market at its busiest. This walk can also be combined with walk 1 to create a circular walk along the north and south banks.

start	Tower Hill Underground Station (Circle and District lines)
nearest postcode	EC3N 1JL
finish	Blackfriars Underground Station (Circle and District lines)
distance	2¼ miles / 3.7 km (4 miles / 6.4 km if combined with walk 1)
time	1¼ hours (2¼ hours if combined with walk 1)
terrain	Surfaced roads and paths; steps to climb and descend; no steep hills.

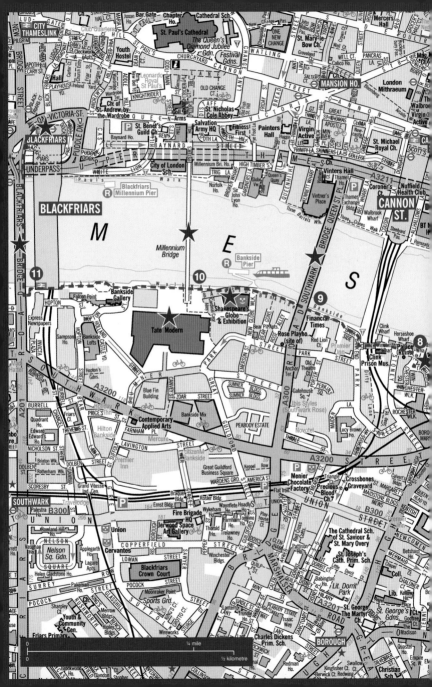

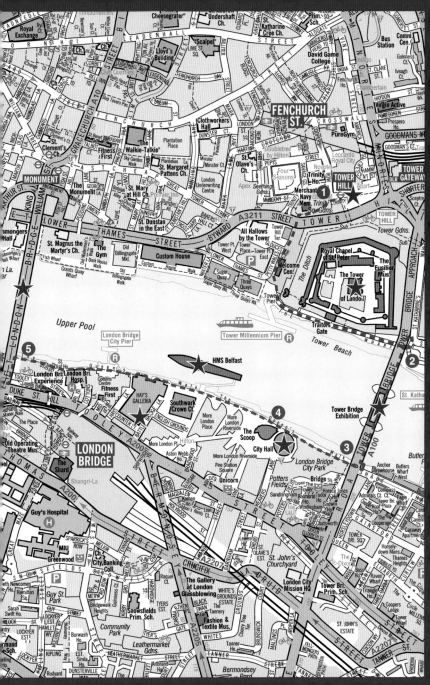

1 If you are starting from Tower Hill Underground Station, cross Trinity Square Gardens diagonally left, cross the road at the traffic lights, and go downhill to turn left along the river and past the Tower of London ★ . If you are continuing along the circular route from Blackfriars (walk 1), follow the river below the Tower.

2 By Dead Man's Hole (a former mortuary for bodies found in the river), climb the stairs to the eastern pavement of Tower Bridge ★ , opened in 1894. The bridge needed to accommodate tall-masted sailing vessels using the Pool of London. The solution was a double drawbridge of two hydraulically operated bascules: state-of-the-art Victorian engineering in pseudo-medieval fancy dress to match the Tower of London. The bridge's next opening times are advertised on its website under 'bridge lift times'.

3 Take the stairs at the south end to pass under the bridge, emerging by City Hall ★ (which has several nicknames, including Darth Vader's Helmet and The Onion), the meeting place of the Greater London Assembly and headquarters of the Mayor of Greater London. Across the river are views to the Tower and many more modern architectural icons, from The Gherkin and The Cheesegrater to The Scalpel and The Walkie-Talkie (See walk 5 for a walk past these buildings.)

4 The arena past City Hall is The Scoop. This area is known as More London. Past HMS Belfast ★ – a 1934 light cruiser that served on Second World War Arctic convoys and saw service in the Korean War, and which is now part of the Imperial War Museum – is Hay's Galleria ★ . Designed as a secure dock for tea clippers, it now contains shops, bistros and a mechanical sculpture called 'The Navigators'.

5 Just before the stairs to London Bridge, look right towards The Monument; this was the line of Old London Bridge. Climb the stairs and turn left. The stone spike commemorates the metal spikes on Old London Bridge where the heads of executed malefactors were displayed.

6 Cross Borough High Street at the traffic lights and descend the steps to Borough Market, a great place to pause for street food or a pub break.

7 Loop right past Southwark Cathedral ★ , a religious foundation for a thousand years and a cathedral since 1905; William Shakespeare's brother Edmund is buried here and John Harvard – founder of Harvard College – was baptized here in 1607. Next comes the full-scale replica of the *Golden Hind* ★ in which the privateer Sir Francis Drake sailed around the world in the 1570s and netted six tonnes of Spanish treasure. This ship, built in 1973, has circled the globe twice.

8 Follow Clink Street round to the left, past the remains of the Bishop of Winchester's great hall and the site of his prison. When he owned this area in late medieval times, it was notorious for its taverns, its theatres, its bear-baiting pits and its eighteen brothels. He even granted the licences to the Bankside prostitutes, which is how they came to be known as 'Winchester Geese'. You will rejoin the Thames after Cannon Street Railway Bridge at The Anchor pub, where 18th-century writer Dr Samuel Johnson used to drink.

9 Pass under Southwark Bridge ★, whose tiled wall panels recall London's great Frost Fairs. Beyond the bridge is a reconstruction of Shakespeare's Globe ★, a working theatre opened in 1997 after a campaign spearheaded by the US-born actor and director, Sam Wanamaker.

10 At the south end of the Millennium Bridge ★, Tate Modern ★ occupies the former Bankside Power Station and houses the Tate Gallery's collection of international modern art. The spectacular Blackfriars Railway Station ahead was redeveloped between 2009 and 2012. It straddles the river along the largest solar-powered bridge in the world, whose 4,400 roof panels provide up to 50 per cent of the station's energy requirements.

11 Pass under the station and climb the steps to Blackfriars Bridge ★. The first bridge here was opened in the 1760s to ease pressure on Old London Bridge and provide a grand entrance to the City. After a century it was replaced by Joseph Cubitt's 'Venetian Gothic' design. The tops of its granite piers resemble pulpits: a reminder that this area is named after the black friars of the Dominican foundation on the north bank. The east side is decorated with estuary plants and birds and the west side with upriver wildlife. Cross the bridge to Blackfriars Station ★ where the walk ends opposite the fantastically eccentric Black Friar pub.

A·Z walk five

Ancient and Modern Architecture in the City

The Tower to The Gherkin.

When William of Normandy came to London in 1066, he quickly began work on three fortifications to protect himself from the Londoners and awe them into submission. Of these, the most important and the only one to survive was the White Tower, which lies at the centre of what we now know as the Tower of London. Over the past thousand years, the Tower has served as a palace, a fortress, a prison, a place of execution, a mint, an observatory and even a menagerie. Today, it guards the Crown Jewels.

This packed circular walk takes in a site of state executions before striking out westward from the Tower to pass by the church of All Hallows by the Tower, which contains an arch from an earlier Anglo-Saxon church on the site. The route continues past the tranquil garden of St Dunstan's Church to The Monument which celebrates London's recovery from the Great Fire of 1666. Here we loop north into the beautifully ornate Leadenhall Market, a market for seven centuries but now an upmarket retail and recreation centre as well as the film location where Harry Potter bought his wand. To complete this architectural odyssey, the route continues past some of the City's most striking (and oddly nicknamed) modern architecture, before returning to Tower Hill via a hidden stretch of Roman wall.

start / finish	Tower Hill Underground Station (Circle and District lines)
nearest postcode	EC3N 1JL
distance	1½ miles / 2.3 km
time	45 minutes
terrain	Surfaced roads and paths; steps to climb and descend; no steep hills.

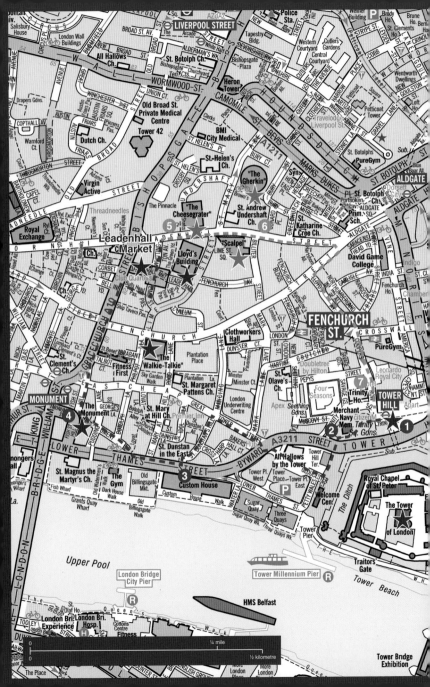

1 By the exit from Tower Hill Station, climb the few steps to the viewpoint above the station where you will find the Tower Hill Sundial. The rim records a witty potted history of London. Descending, cross Trinity Square Gardens towards the two Mercantile Marine memorials. Just beyond these, tucked modestly away and easy to miss, is the site of the Tower Hill scaffold where, between 1381 and 1780, more than 100 people were executed. Beheaded here before crowds of several thousand were Thomas More, Thomas Cromwell and the Duke of Monmouth.

2 Crossing the main road at the lights, walk towards the river past the ticket offices to see the pepperpot turrets of the White Tower. Turn right into Gloucester Court and pass All Hallows Church, whose crypt houses a fascinating small museum, to cross at the lights on Byward Street. After reading the plaque on The Hung, Drawn and Quartered pub, go right and immediately left into Great Tower Street. Ahead on the right is 20 Fenchurch Street, better known as The Walkie-Talkie ★ . Turn left into St Dunstan's Hill to pass the ruined church with its fine Wren Tower. It is now a lush garden.

3 At the foot of the hill, go right along Lower Thames Street, passing Custom House and Old Billingsgate Market across the street. Crossing St Mary at Hill, bear right along Monument Street. Ahead, past Pudding Lane where the Great Fire of London started in a baker's shop, The Monument ★ , the tallest freestanding column in the world, is surmounted by a flaming urn in bronze. If it fell towards Pudding Lane the urn would land where the fire began. It was intended to be a great telescope, but the London skies proved too smoky.

4 Turn right up Fish Street Hill, and take the double light-controlled crossing onto the right side of Gracechurch Street straight ahead. Crossing over Fenchurch Street at the lights, continue to the narrow Bulls Head Passage on the right. Turn left at the end of this and into the ornate and much filmed Leadenhall Market ★ (Diagon Alley to Harry Potter fans). You are walking through the forum of the huge Roman basilica or town hall. Continue straight, past the racks where poultry was once displayed, and at the end of Whittington Avenue turn right into Leadenhall Street.

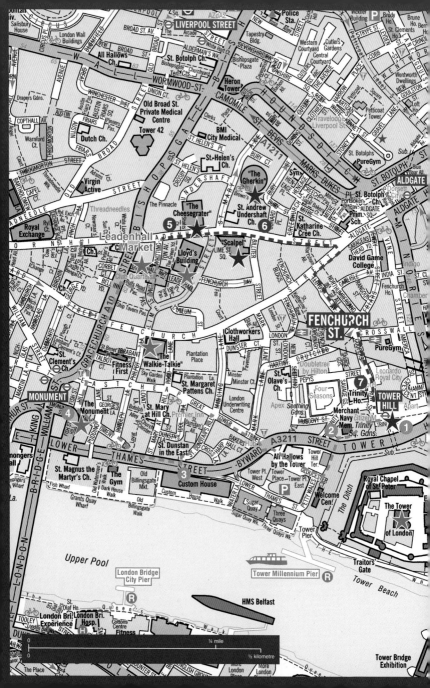

5 Pause at Lime Street. On the right is the innovative Lloyd's Building ★ by Richard Rogers, with all the services on the outside for easy maintenance and replacement. Lloyd's, which has even insured against the discovery of the Loch Ness Monster, was founded in a coffee house, and its red-coated porters are still called waiters. On the other side of Leadenhall Street, dwarfed by The Gherkin ★ (the building at 30 St Mary Axe), is St Andrew Undershaft. A huge maypole used to stand here on Mayday, and a smaller replica shelters opposite under the Leadenhall Building ('The Cheesegrater') ★ . On the other side of Lime Street you will pass the building whose nickname 'The Scalpel' ★ has now been adopted as its official name.

6 Continue along Leadenhall Street. Past St Katharine Cree Church, at the junction of Leadenhall Street and Fenchurch Street, cross Fenchurch Street at the lights by Aldgate Pump and turn right. Walk as far as Lloyds Avenue, where you turn left. Follow the avenue to cross Crutched Friars and Crosswall into Coopers Row. Along Coopers Row on the right is the side of Trinity House, the lighthouse authority for the coast of England, Wales and the Channel Islands; its Masters have included Samuel Pepys and the late Duke of Edinburgh.

7 Opposite Trinity House, turn into the car park of The Leonardo Royal London City. Ahead is a stretch of London's city wall, preserved by having been incorporated into a warehouse. At the foot of the wall, identifiable by the courses of red brick and tile every few feet up the structure, are the remains of the Roman wall. Go back onto Coopers Row and turn left to return to Tower Hill Station.

AZ walk six

Blood, Guts and Body Snatchers

The deadly history of Smithfield.

Smithfield, a medieval 'smooth field' large and flat enough for the sport of jousting (hence the name of Giltspur Street), began as a horse market. Eventually, butchery took over the area and it became home to London Central Markets (better known as Smithfield Market), one of the largest meat markets in Europe. Butchery of a different kind took place in West Smithfield, which was for centuries the site of public executions. The Scottish national hero William Wallace was hanged, drawn and quartered here in 1305, religious martyrs were burned alive and poisoners were boiled. Smithfield was even a centre of the body-snatching trade, whose lasting legacy is the watch-house built to guard Holy Sepulchre's graveyard.

The route of this circular walk takes us past the Central Criminal Court (the Old Bailey). For 800 years, until 1902, this was the site of Newgate Prison, outside of which public hangings took place between 1783 and 1869. From here we pass St Bartholomew's Hospital (Barts), once part of a priory founded here in 1123. The church of St Bartholomew the Great, with its rare Norman features, was formerly its chapel. After Smithfield Market, we continue to Farringdon Station, opened in 1863 as the eastern terminus of the world's first underground railway, and return to St Paul's Station via St John's Gate, once gateway to the Priory of St John of Jerusalem.

The market has attracted many exceptional pubs to the area should you wish to pause your walk for refreshment.

start / finish	St Paul's Underground Station (Central line)
nearest postcode	EC2V 6AA
distance	2 miles / 3.2 km
time	1 hour
terrain	Surfaced roads and paths; steps to climb and descend; no steep hills.

This Boy is
in Memmory Put up
for the late FIRE of
LONDON
Occasion'd by the
Sin of Gluttony
1666

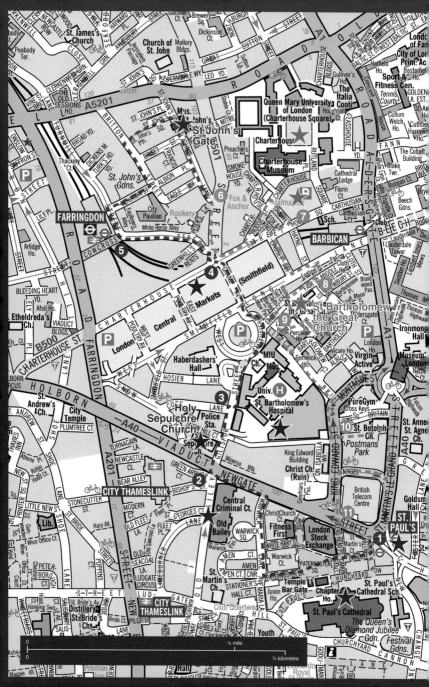

1 From Panyer Alley beside St Paul's Underground Station ★ , walk towards St Paul's Cathedral ★ and turn right along Paternoster Row into Paternoster Square. Once occupied by makers of rosary beads, this area later became a centre of bookselling and publishing. Ahead, Paternoster Lane leads to Ave Maria Lane. Cross the road and turn right past Amen Court. These street names recall religious processions around the cathedral. After Cutler's Hall, turn left into Newgate Street and cross Old Bailey to look back to the Central Criminal Court ★ on your right and across to Holy Sepulchre Church on your left.

2 Cross Holborn Viaduct. To the right is the gloriously ornate Viaduct Tavern, which claims to be the City's most haunted pub. Continue past the watch-house to the corner of Cock Lane, where 19th-century body snatchers sold 'resurrected' bodies for dissection. This was Pie Corner, where the Great Fire of London ended in 1666. Look up to see the statue of the chubby Golden Boy. This recalls a belief that the fire, which started in Pudding Lane, was divine retribution for London's gluttony.

3 Crossing Giltspur Street, pass the hospital gateway to enter West Smithfield; notice the memorials to William Wallace, the Protestant Martyrs and The Peasants' Revolt. At the church gatehouse, bear left to cross Long Lane into Smithfield Market's Grand Avenue. When divorces were rare and hugely expensive, a man could sell his wife here if he observed all the usual regulations!

4 At the pedestrian crossing, cross Charterhouse Street, bearing left into Cowcross Street. Just before Farringdon Station, notice the pawnbroker's sign outside The Castle. King George IV once pawned his watch here and granted the pub a pawnbroker's licence in perpetuity.

5 Go right into Turnmill Street, and right again into Benjamin Street before turning left into Britton Street. At The Jerusalem Tavern, take St John's Path, to the right, through St John's Square, and turn right down St John's Lane through the former gateway to the Priory of St John of Jerusalem ★ . William Shakespeare knew this as the office of Elizabeth I's Master of the Revels; later, the father of William Hogarth, the artist and social critic, ran it as a coffee house where only Latin was spoken.

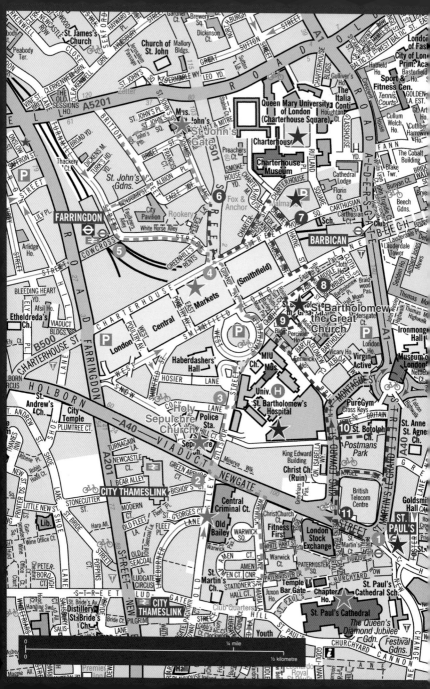

6 Continue into St John Street, where you turn right and walk to the end of the road. Turn left into Charterhouse Street, bearing left into Charterhouse Square ★, which began as a Black Death burial ground and developed into a Carthusian monastery, later suppressed by Henry VIII. Christ Church School was founded here, and today the surviving buildings are an almshouse.

7 Leave by the gateway, and turn right past Hayne Street, left along Lindsey Street, and left again along Long Lane. At The Old Red Cow pub, take the passageway to emerge facing The Hand and Shears pub. To the right is a road named Cloth Fair. Bartholomew Fair was held around here to boost the English cloth industry and fund St Bartholomew's Priory, but it became so riotous that it was closed down in 1855.

8 Along Cloth Fair, climb the steps by the far end of the church to enter the graveyard of St Bartholomew the Great ★. Notice how centuries of burials have raised the churchyard above the west door.

9 Taking the further steps down to the passageway beneath, turn right through the gatehouse and left into Little Britain. Follow the road right into King Edward Street until you see a gate on the left leading into Postman's Park, a onetime burial ground close to London's former chief post office. Here the artist G. F. Watts founded a memorial to ordinary people of extraordinary bravery.

10 Walk through the park into Aldersgate Street, turn right towards St Paul's, bear right into Angel Street, and follow King Edward Street left as far as the ruins of Christ Church Greyfriars. The interior was destroyed in the Blitz in 1940, but the garden planting recalls its features.

11 Cross Newgate Street and head left to return to Panyer Alley.

AZ walk seven

London's Melting Pot

Spitalfields in the East End.

This circular walk, best done on a Sunday, explores one of London's most culturally diverse and exciting districts. The area first came to prominence as a great Roman cemetery, situated just outside the city walls of Londinium and along an important route to the north.

Around 1197, the Hospital of St Mary-without-Bishopsgate was founded, known as St Mary Spital. The fields around it were Spital Fields; hence the area's name today. The hospital was part of a priory that was closed in 1539 during the Dissolution of the Monasteries, after which the site was built over. By the 1700s, Spitalfields was a suburb of the city.

The east of London has been welcoming newcomers for centuries. The word 'refugee' was coined here to describe the Huguenots: French Protestants who fled to Britain in the late 1600s to escape religious persecution, establishing Spitalfields as a centre for luxury silk production. In the 19th century, thousands of Jews fleeing ruthless pogroms in Eastern Europe poured into the area, joining the small Jewish community that had settled here in the 1650s. During the 20th century, immigrants from Bangladesh found work in the garment industry just as their Huguenot and Jewish predecessors had, but they also used their culinary skills to turn Brick Lane into London's 'Curry Mile'.

start / finish	Liverpool Street Station (Central, Circle, Hammersmith & City, Metropolitan, London Overground, National Rail and TfL lines)
nearest postcode	EC2M 7PP
distance	2¼ miles / 3.7 km
time	1 hour
terrain	Surfaced roads and paths; optional steps to descend and climb; no steep hills.

1 At the Hope Square exit from Liverpool Street Station ★ is a statue commemorating the children of Sir Nicholas Winton's Kindertransport scheme who arrived at the station between 1938–9 while escaping from Nazi persecution. It was made by Frank Meisler, one of 669 children saved. From Hope Square, turn right along Liverpool Street.

2 Turn left and follow Old Broad Street to go left again under the arch in the building and into Bishopsgate Churchyard. Passing the fanciful 1895 Turkish bath, you come to St. Botolph church hall with its two figures of charity school children. Leaving the churchyard, turn right and cross Bishopsgate to Heron Tower.

3 Look back to see the metal shape of a bishop's mitre set into the wall opposite Heron Tower, marking the site of the city gate rebuilt by a 7th-century Bishop of London and named after him. With St Botolph on your left, follow Bishopsgate as far as the police station. The City of London police uniform is subtly different from that of Metropolitan police officers, and the City force specializes in combating terrorism and financial crime. Continue to Dirty Dicks, a 200-year-old pub named after Nathaniel Bentley, whose fiancée died on their wedding eve. Brokenhearted, he locked himself away to spend his days in squalor on this site.

4 After Dirty Dicks, turn right down Middlesex Street, still unofficially known as Petticoat Lane. Huguenot and Jewish traders established a market here, which continues every day except Saturday. Take the left fork into Widegate Street and look up at the figures inset at first-floor level, which once advertised a baker's shop.

5 Go left along Sandys Row, whose synagogue was formerly a Huguenot church, and turn right to follow Artillery Lane; there was an artillery ground here where archers and gunners practised. Number 56 was a splendid 18th-century shop retailing silks.

6 At the corner, the building on the left was Providence Row Night Refuge and Convent, run for a century by the Sisters of Mercy. Turn right down Bell Lane and left into Brune Street, where the 1902 'Soup Kitchen for the Jewish Poor' provides another reminder of the area's past privations. At Toynbee Street turn left.

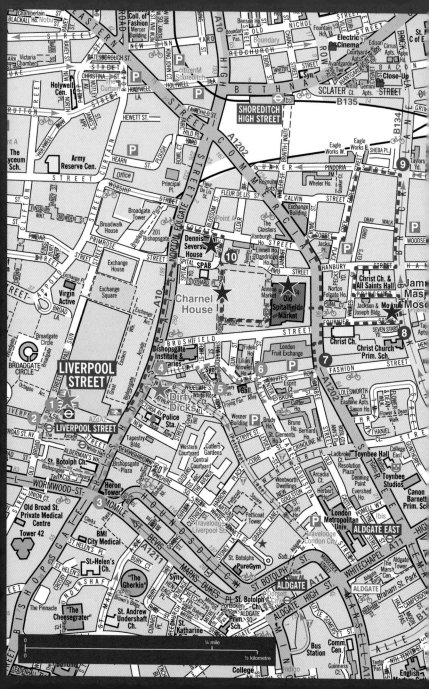

7 Continue onto Commercial Street and cross the road opposite Nicholas Hawksmoor's dominating Christ Church. Turn right into Fournier Street. The tall houses were built by Huguenot weavers. Their looms were at the top where large windows made the most of the available light. By the late 1800s these houses were in multiple occupation. Towards the end of Fournier Street, S. Schwartz's shop gives a flavour of the street's past, and on the corner is the Jamme Masjid Mosque ★ , formerly a church and a synagogue. This area is the centre of 'Banglatown' (see the street signs) where many Bangladeshi people settled when they moved to Britain in the late 20th century.

8 Turn left into Brick Lane, famous for its many curry houses, and left again into Princelet Street, where number 19, once a synagogue, is now the Museum of Immigration and Diversity. This area is full of street art. Take a double-right turn into Hanbury Street and back in Brick Lane turn left through the Truman Brewery site, now an entertainment complex.

9 Turn left into Quaker Street and left again into Grey Eagle Street. Continue through Corbet Place to join Commercial Road. Go left to the Ten Bells pub and cross to Old Spitalfields Market ★ , once a fruit and vegetable market and now a food and fashion hotspot with a regular Sunday market. Walk through the market into sculpture-packed Bishop's Square, site of a huge archeological dig around St Mary Spital and a vast neighbouring burial site. Some finds are displayed amongst the paving, and there are steps down to the charnel house ★ if you wish to see it.

10 Leave via Spital Square and turn left into Folgate Street with Dennis Severs' House ★ (an imaginative recreation of a Spitalfields house over 200 years) on the left. At the end of Folgate Street, walk left to return down Bishopsgate to Liverpool Street Station.

▲Z walk eight

Curiouser and Curiouser

Intriguing oddities around the tranquil Inns of Court.

This weekday morning walk leads us through three of the four remaining Inns of Court: Inner Temple, Middle Temple and Lincoln's Inn (the fourth being Gray's Inn). For over 600 years these 'inns' have been where advocates known as barristers train, qualify and go on to practise their profession from offices still referred to as 'chambers'. From simple lodgings housing established barristers and their pupils, the Inns of Court have developed into imposing complexes of buildings laid out like Oxford and Cambridge colleges.

The Knights Templar, an order of soldier-priests who pledged to protect pilgrims to the Holy Land, originally occupied this area. After the order was suppressed, its lands, including Temple Church, passed to the lawyers of Inner and Middle Temple. Lincoln's Inn is a similarly ancient foundation, named after a prominent patron.

This circular walk takes us past some of the intriguing curiosities of this area including a silver mousetrap, two cherubs making a telephone call, and a statue with a private income.

start / finish	Temple Underground Station (Circle and District lines)
nearest postcode	WC2R 2PH
distance	1½ miles / 2.4 km
time	45 minutes
terrain	Surfaced roads and paths; steps to climb and descend; no steep hills, one unsurfaced path.

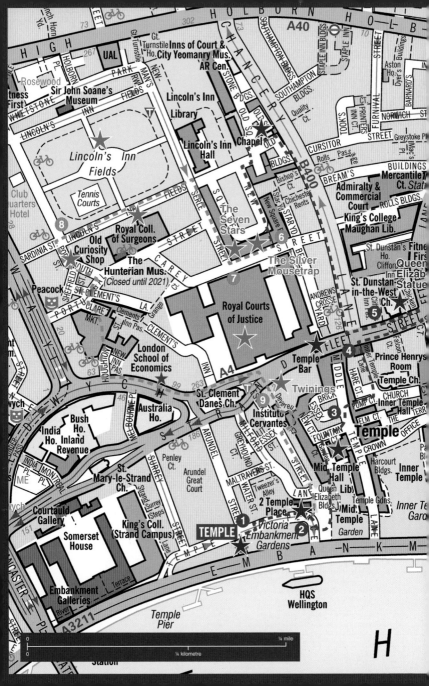

1 Outside Temple Station ★, facing the unfamiliar 1932 London Underground map to the right of the entrance, turn right and climb the steps. At the traffic lights to the right, cross the road and continue right to the gates of 2 Temple Place ★. Beside the building, one lamp standard shows two cherubs making a call on an early telephone; the second has one cherub turning a generator which powers a light bulb held by the other.

2 Further along Temple Place is a gate. Go through this and cross diagonally to a flight of steps leading into Temple. Across the gardens to your right you will see the Middle Temple arms, the Lamb and Flag; the symbol of Inner Temple is the winged horse Pegasus. Continue to Fountain Court, and turn right to face Middle Temple Hall ★. The present hall dates from 1573, and Shakespeare's *Twelfth Night* was first performed here in 1601 before Queen Elizabeth I.

3 Beyond the Hall, cross Middle Temple Lane. Take Pump Court to your left towards Temple Church, consecrated in 1185 and said to be modelled on the Church of the Holy Sepulchre in Jerusalem. Skirting the left end of the church, follow Inner Temple Lane uphill into Fleet Street.

4 Turn right past the signs of Gosling's Bank (squirrels) and Hoare's Bank (a golden bottle), inevitable companions of the legal system. Cross at the Fetter Lane traffic lights, and go left to St Dunstan in the West Church. The statue of Queen Elizabeth I ★ on the wall was left £700 by the suffragist Dame Millicent Fawcett for its upkeep.

5 Continue, and opposite the 17th-century Prince Henry's Rooms, cross the road to turn right up Chancery Lane, passing London's oldest tailors, Ede & Ravenscroft (1689), which specializes in lawyers' wigs and gowns, as well as Coronation robes. Pass King's College Library, cross Carey Street, and, after Chichester Rents and Bishop's Court, take the gateway left into Lincoln's Inn. Go right behind the Old Hall to reach the undercroft of the chapel ★, where, during the 18th century, abandoned babies were left to be raised by the Inn. Pass left through the undercroft and walk left down the nearer side of New Square through the gate into Carey Street.

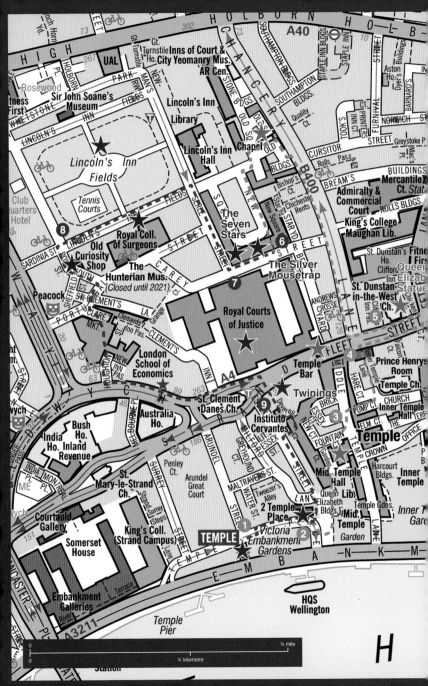

6 On your right a sign reads 'The Silver Mousetrap' ★, in honour of the mousetraps sold on this site in the past. Eighteenth-century ladies wore elaborate wigs powdered with flour; when these were laid aside at night a silver mousetrap was a must-have accessory to stop them from being eaten. Turn right to pass The Seven Stars pub. Not only is the window display jaw-dropping, but the pub is presided over by a cat dressed every day in a white, starched ruff. Opposite The Seven Stars is the rear of The Royal Courts of Justice ★ (the Law Courts), opened by Queen Victoria in 1882. The building is made up of 35 million bricks, and contains three and a half miles (5.6 km) of corridors and a thousand-plus rooms

7 Continue to Serle Street and turn right. By the gateway to Lincoln's Inn, cross to the south side of Lincoln's Inn Fields ★, London's largest square. To the left is the Royal College of Surgeons ★, whose collection includes the brain of the computer pioneer Charles Babbage and Sir Winston Churchill's denture.

8 At Portsmouth Street, turn left past The Old Curiosity Shop – a 16th-century house that survived the slum clearance in the late 1800s – and then right into Portugal Street. At Clare Market, go left through the London School of Economics and right down Houghton Street into Aldwych. Bear left, and after St Clement Dane's Church cross the Strand by the zebra crossing. Look back at the splendid façade of the Law Courts and left at the less popular Temple Bar memorial ★ in the middle of the road, marking the boundary between Westminster and the City of London. A sovereign wishing to enter the City is met here by the Lord Mayor with a ceremonial sword, who offers the City's protection.

9 Go right and pass Twinings, whose tea is advertised by two Chinese figures above the doorway, then turn left through Devereux Court into Essex Street. Walk left to the end of Essex Street. Here stairs lead down to Temple Place. Turn right to return to the start.

▲Z walk nine

West End Culture

Theatre, shopping and elegance around the Strand.

Westminster began its rise to significance in the 1040s when Edward the Confessor established his palace here. As centre of the royal court, and later of Parliament, it attracted wealthy and influential individuals, and the riverbank or 'strand' became lined with fine palaces. After the Great Fire of 1666, the area was developed to accommodate the professional classes and minor gentry.

Street names reflect this story. The Duke of Buckingham, selling York House in 1672 for housing, stipulated that the new streets should bear his full name as George Street, Villiers Street, Duke Street, Of Alley (now York Place), and Buckingham Street. Later developers, the Scottish Adams brothers, have left us Robert Street, Adam Street and John Adam Street.

Parts of the district acquired a bohemian and lawless side, and by the later 19th century the fringes of the Strand had declined into a criminal slum. Now the West End is a centre of culture and retail, and Covent Garden is regarded as chic.

This circular walk leads us through streets of elegant houses to the bustle of the Strand, passing the glitzy Savoy Hotel, Somerset House, London's oldest restaurant, some fine theatres and all the excitement of Covent Garden.

start / finish	Embankment Underground Station (Bakerloo, Circle and District lines)
nearest postcode	WC2N 6NS
distance	1½ miles / 2.5 km
time	1 hour
terrain	Surfaced roads and paths; steps to climb and descend; no steep hills.

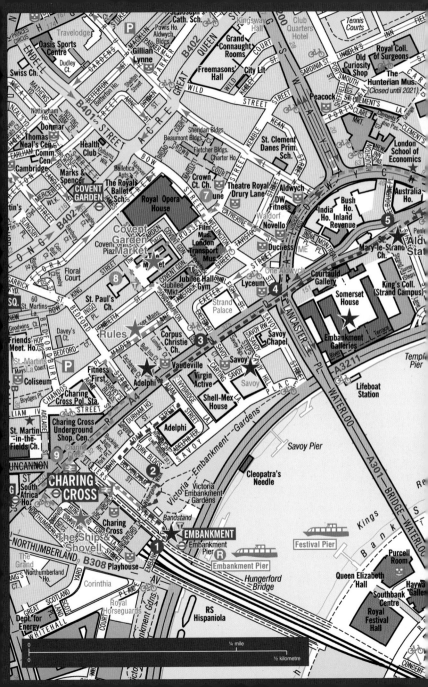

① Take the Villiers Street exit from Embankment Underground Station and walk up the right-hand pavement to the entrance of Victoria Embankment Gardens. Ahead on your left is York Watergate, last vestige of the Strand's great mansions.

② Climb the steps behind it into Buckingham Street, which housed at various times Charles Dickens, Samuel Taylor Coleridge, Samuel Pepys and Peter the Great. Continue to John Adam Street and turn right. Just before the junction with Adam Street is the imposing Royal Society of Arts. Cross Adam Street to the left and continue up the road. Opposite the Adelphi Theatre ★, one of just three survivals of the dozens of theatres and music halls that once lined the street, go right, along the Strand.

③ Just past Carting Lane, with its lamp standard fuelled by sewer gas, is The Coal Hole, whose bar celebrates the Wolf Club, established nearby for married men forbidden to sing in the bath! Next comes the entrance to the Savoy Hotel ★ and Theatre: the only London street where traffic must drive on the right. The hotel, named after the Duke of Lancaster's palace destroyed in the Peasants' Revolt of 1381, was built on the proceeds of Richard D'Oyley Carte's Gilbert and Sullivan operas. The topiary at the entrance depicts Kaspar, the carved cat brought in whenever thirteen people sit down to dine. Continue to Simpson's, a restaurant which started as a 'home of chess' and a 'cigar divan'. Savoy Street further along on the right leads to the 16th-century Savoy Chapel.

④ Cross Lancaster Place and walk on to Somerset House ★ on your right, now an important cultural centre. Opposite is the island church of St Mary le Strand.

⑤ Past King's College London is the disused Aldwych Underground Station ★, which now makes more money (from filming and tours) than it did when it was operating. Cross Surrey Street and Arundel Street. Then cross the Strand to St Clement Dane's, the Royal Air Force church.

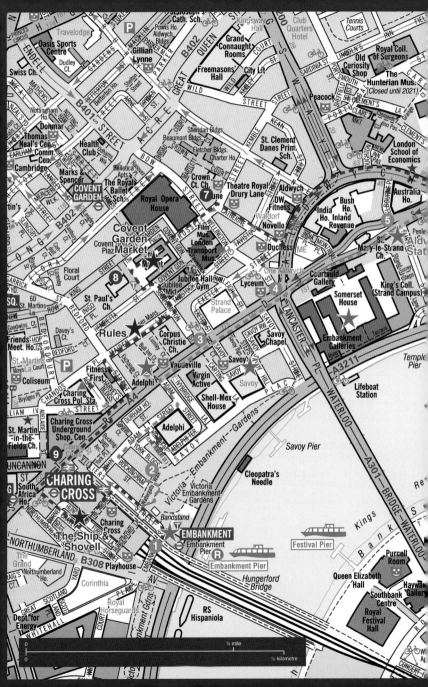

6 Proceed to the north side of the Strand. After the Romans left Britain, the area between here and Trafalgar Square became an Anglo-Saxon settlement. Turn left and walk around Aldwych, passing on your left Australia House (Gringotts Bank to Harry Potter fans), Bush House (formerly headquarters of the BBC World Service) and India House. After crossing Kingsway and Drury Lane, turn right up Catherine Street. This district was notorious in the 1700s for its gin shops and brothels, and a century later it was one of London's worst slums.

7 Opposite the Theatre Royal, go left across Wellington Street, passing the Royal Opera House, and enter Covent Garden ★. Originally a convent garden supplying the monks of Westminster, it was owned in the 1630s by the Duke of Bedford, who commissioned an arcaded Italianate square of fine houses. The duke later introduced a fruit, vegetable and flower market which eventually took over the area until it moved out in 1974. Walk through the market to Inigo Jones's church of St Paul, where in 1660 Samuel Pepys watched a Punch and Judy show. Street entertainers still perform here.

8 Walk left from the church, and cross Henrietta Street into Southampton Street. Turn right into Maiden Lane, passing Rules ★, London's oldest restaurant, where King Edward VII dined his mistresses. Cross Bedford Street, and turn left towards the Strand. Turn right at the end, and cross the Strand at the Agar Street traffic lights. Then turn right to cross Villiers Street, and the taxi entrance to Charing Cross Station. To your left is a Victorian reconstruction of a late 13th-century cross which once stood nearby. Continue across the taxi exit towards Trafalgar Square.

9 Turn left into Craven Street. After Benjamin Franklin's House, turn left into Craven Passage to pass The Ship & Shovell ★, the only London pub on both sides of a road. Go down the steps and walk through The Arches under the station to emerge in Villiers Street. Turn right to return to Embankment Station.

A–Z walk ten

London's Lost Docks

History and regeneration in Wapping and Shadwell.

By the late 18th century, London was the busiest port in the world, but was struggling to cope with the volume of shipping. Ships often waited weeks to be unloaded and frequently fell victim to river pirates. The lightermen who ferried cargo to shore also often helped themselves along the way.

To counter crime on the river, the Marine Police Force, later the Thames Division of the Metropolitan Police, was formed in 1798. A year later, planning began for the first of London's purpose-built docks.

This walk begins near St Katharine Docks, opened in 1828. Dug on the site of a huge slum, ruthlessly cleared, the new, secure dock, surrounded by a high wall, specialized in luxury goods, from marble and ivory to spices, wines and perfume. It could hold 120 ships, and cargo was unloaded by crane straight into tall warehouses. Downriver, in Wapping, the earlier London Docks, opened in 1805, have largely been filled in, but St Katharine Docks, scene of a disastrous fire in the Second World War, have been reborn as a glamorous marina.

This circular walk takes in Wapping and Shadwell, two districts whose story is closely bound up with the river and its trade, and where, despite gentrification, much of the flavour of the old docklands remains.

start / finish	Tower Hill Underground Station (Circle and District lines)
nearest postcode	EC3N 1JL
distance	3 miles / 5 km
time	1 hour 45 minutes
terrain	Surfaced roads and paths; steps to descend; no steep hills.

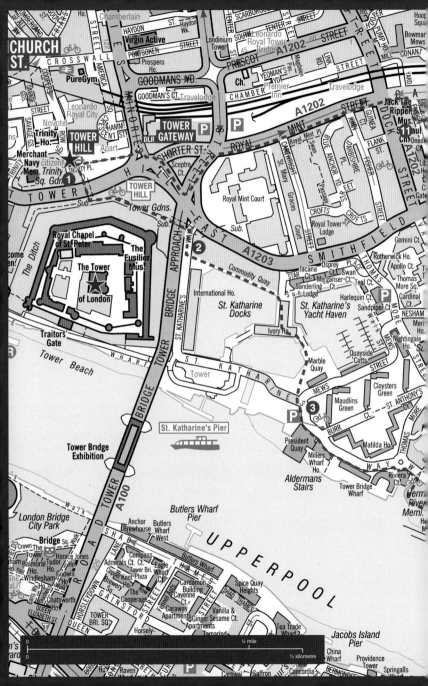

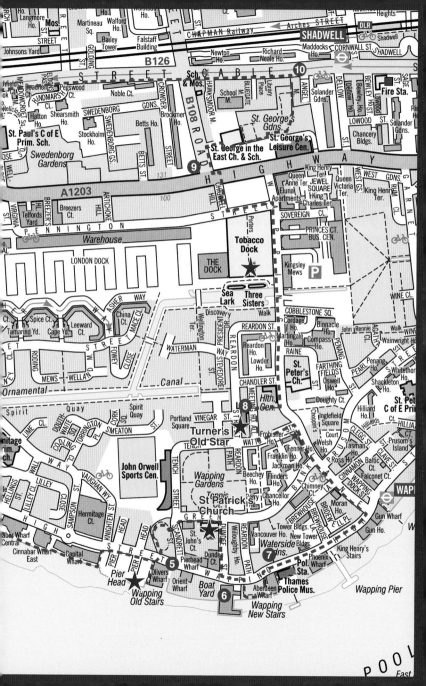

1 From the exit of Tower Hill Station ★ turn left and loop right to descend the stairway towards the Tower of London ★. Pass under the road and go left beside the old moat. The subway ahead has some helpful information about the area. Leaving the subway, go right and then left into St Katharine Docks.

2 Follow the marina shore, and go right to Ivory House. Through the archway, turn left and take the bridge to Marble Quay. Cross diagonally right to leave the docks.

3 Along St Katharine's Way, follow a sign pointing right to the Thames Path. This stretch of embankment has fine views upriver through Tower Bridge. Go left, and, at the end of the path, loop right into Hermitage Riverside Memorial Garden. The Dove of Peace commemorates the East Enders who died in the bombing of London's docks during the Second World War.

4 Continue left along the riverside. Where the path ends, a left turn takes you into Wapping High Street, which once had thirty-six pubs and countless brothels. On the right, Pier Head, flanked by two handsome Georgian houses, marks the former entrance to the London Docks. Next comes The Town of Ramsgate, named after the Ramsgate fishing boats that used to anchor nearby. The pub provides food, but, even if you don't go in, walk down the neighbouring alley to Wapping Old Stairs ★, one of hundreds of places from which Thames watermen picked up and set down passengers.

5 Returning to the High Street, cross the road to enter the old churchyard opposite. See on the right the charity school with its figures of a girl and boy. Leaving the churchyard, pause to read the board on The Turk's Head before following Green Bank past St Patrick's Church ★. Many of the Irish labourers who dug the docks stayed on as dockers. Originally, they had no Catholic church. St Patrick's was built in 1879 from their penny-a-week contributions. Past the church, turn right down Dundee Street.

6 After taking in the overhead walkways linking the warehouses on the right so that goods could be moved securely, look ahead to the Metropolitan Police Boatyard, where police boats are maintained and repaired. Cross to enter the neighbouring gardens. On the foreshore close to here was Execution Dock, where pirates were first hanged and then staked out on the foreshore until three tides had passed over them. Their bodies were afterwards displayed on gibbets along the riverside as a warning to others.

7 Returning to Wapping High Street, walk on past warehouses converted into pricey apartments, and turn left along Wapping Lane. At Wapping Green, go left towards Turner's Old Star pub ★ , where notices set out the building's history and its link to witchcraft. Stop here for refreshments if you wish.

8 Take Meeting House Alley to the end of the Green, and turn right to return to Wapping Lane, where you go left past St Peter's Church to cross the bridge. On your left are two replica pirate ships intended as a children's adventure experience in the 1990s. Walk on along the side of Tobacco Dock ★ , and turn left down Pennington Street to peer through the gates into the scarcely used interior. To the right, the statue of a boy and a tiger recalls the killing of a child by a tiger that had escaped from a local menagerie. Continue along Pennington Street and turn right up Chigwell Hill to The Highway, where there are traffic lights to your left.

9 Cross The Highway to the right-hand pavement of Cannon Street Road. Turn into St George's Gardens, and go right and left around St George in the East Church. Cross the gardens and take the exit left into Cable Street by the huge mural depicting the Battle of Cable Street. The text by the mural explains how Oswald Moseley's Fascist march was turned back by a group of dockers and local Jewish residents in 1936.

10 Go left along Cable Street with splendid views right to the City skyscrapers. Reaching Fletcher Street, go left towards the old mission building and right along Wellclose Square into Graces Alley. Wilton's Music Hall ★ on the right has been saved from demolition and is back in business.

11 Turn right up Ensign Street and left along Cable Street across Dock Street. Continue along Royal Mint Street to join Mansell Street. To the left, near the gates of the old Mint building, a series of traffic-light-controlled crossings will take you across Mansell Street, Shorter Street and Minories back to Tower Hill Station.

ᴬZ walk eleven

The Pool of London

Upriver from Rotherhithe to London Bridge.

Starting close to the site from which, in 1620, the Pilgrim Fathers left London on the *Mayflower* bound for the Americas, this walk follows the south bank of the River Thames upriver. Along the way, we pass the entrance to Marc and Isambard Brunel's Thames Tunnel, the first tunnel under a navigable river, and move on to a waterside church where Prince Lee Boo is buried. He had been brought back from the Pacific island where one of the East India Company's ships had, in 1783, been wrecked and repaired, to be given an English education.

We continue past a historic pub and the remains of a royal manor house to cross a river named after a hangman's noose and Jacob's Island, where the villainous Bill Sikes hanged himself in Charles Dickens' *Oliver Twist*. After a stretch of upmarket riverside restaurants, the route takes us under Tower Bridge to enter an exciting new development, More London, before finishing at London Bridge Station.

start	Rotherhithe Rail Station (London Overground Line)
nearest postcode	SE16 4LD
finish	London Bridge Station
	(Jubilee and Northern lines, National Rail)
distance	2 miles / 3 km
time	1 hour
terrain	Surfaced roads and paths; steps to climb and descend; no steep hills.

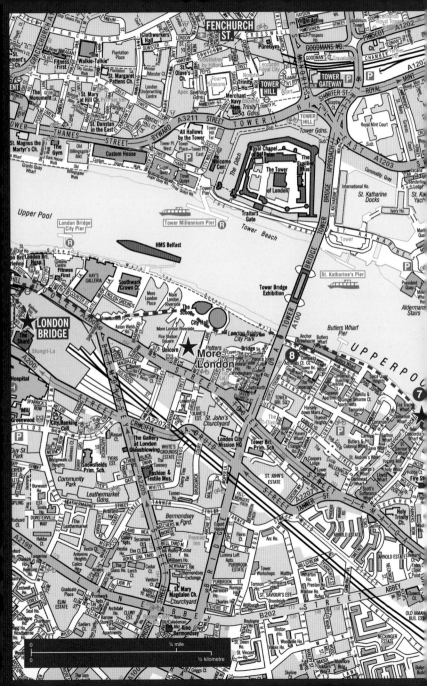

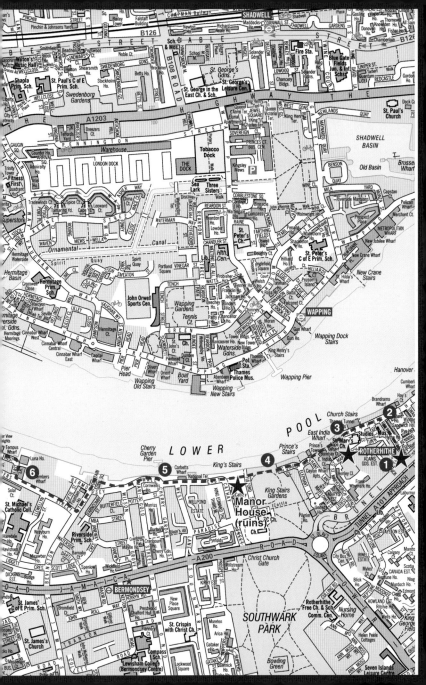

1 Leaving Rotherhithe Station, turn left and left again down Railway Avenue. The artwork on your left shows what the children of Albion Primary School would take on a Victorian railway journey. Approaching the Thames, you pass the shaft of the Thames Tunnel, the world's most popular visitor attraction when it opened in 1843. Its engine house is now the Brunel Museum. The tunnel itself now carries the London Overground between Rotherhithe and Wapping.

2 Past the museum, turn left along Rotherhithe Street, part of the Thames Path which you will follow as far as Tower Bridge. On your right is The Mayflower. This former seafarers' pub flies the Stars and Stripes to celebrate its connection with the Pilgrim Fathers. A little further, St Mary's Church ★ lies on your left, with Prince Lee Boo's tomb outside. At the far end of the churchyard, you will see the site of a free school founded in 1613 by two local sailors, and a building that once housed the parish fire engine and watch-house.

3 Returning to Rotherhithe Street, continue to the point where a sign directs you right and then left along the Thames Path, where you get your first sight of Tower Bridge. Across the river is the blue-and-white boatyard of the Thames Police. Upriver in the Pool of London, there is a speed limit on river craft. This ends at the boatyard, and you will see craft suddenly accelerating here.

4 At King's Stairs Gardens, go down the steps and turn right past The Angel, an unspoilt pub with a river terrace. There is an informative notice on the side of the pub. Just past The Angel, lie the ruins of King Edward III's medieval Manor House ★ , and by the river wall is a sculpted family group (including the cat): *Dr Salter's Daydream*. Rotherhithe and Bermondsey went into decline in the 1800s when the new docks and industrialized shipyards decimated traditional riverside trades, and by the early 20th century they were desperately poor districts. The information by the sculpture group spells out how the inspirational Alfred and Ada Salter made a difference.

5 Reaching Angel Wharf, return to the riverside along the walkway running parallel to Bermondsey Wall East. After briefly rejoining the roadway, return to the river path until you reach Fountain Green Square, where the Thames Path goes inland and then right along Chambers Street. The mural here celebrates London's new super-sewer, the Thames Tideway Tunnel, 15½ miles (25 km) long and 26½ feet (7.2 metres) in diameter, which partly replaces Joseph Bazalgette's magnificent Victorian sewage system.

6 Turn right down East Lane, where the Thames Path continues, and left along Bermondsey Wall West. Reaching a white wall on your right, cross to the riverside to see the barge gardens of the houseboats moored here. Continue to the left turn into Mill Street, where the Thames Path takes a right turn leading to St Saviour's Dock Bridge ★ across the River Neckinger, which is thought to take its name from 'the Devil's neckerchief', the hangman's noose. Jacob's Island was here when the river ran red from Bermondsey's leather trade, and piracy flourished.

7 After the information board, follow the Thames, with fine views half-right over the City. The river frontage here bristles with smart bars and restaurants. Past Le Pont de la Tour, go left to Shad Thames. Look left to the overhead walkways linking the repurposed warehouses, before turning right towards Tower Bridge.

8 Pass under Tower Bridge and continue into Potters Field Park at the start of the More London development ★ , which stretches from here to London Bridge. Go left around City Hall with the Scoop amphitheatre and the water feature to the right, and head down More London Place with The Shard ahead. At Tooley Street, cross to the entrance of London Bridge Mainline Station ★ . For London Bridge Underground Station, continue right to Joiner Street.

AZ walk twelve

Palaces, Parliament and Power

The City of Westminster.

Westminster has been a centre of royal, political and religious life for a thousand years. In the 1040s, King Edward the Confessor began transforming the monastery church of St Peter into a magnificent abbey, establishing Westminster Palace nearby. This burned down in 1512. By 1530 Henry VIII was developing the sprawling Palace of Whitehall with a tiltyard for jousting and a hunting ground (now Horse Guards and St James's Park). In 1691, when this too was largely destroyed by fire, the royal court shifted to St James's Palace, until Queen Victoria moved into Buckingham Palace in 1837.

Parliament got its own building, Westminster Hall, in 1399, as power gradually transferred from the Crown. The present Houses of Parliament replace those destroyed in a fire in 1834, which spared Westminster Hall.

Westminster Abbey is not only a place of worship, but a meeting ground for Church and State. Coronations and important national events are celebrated here, and burials and memorials include not just monarchs but also great commoners, including the Unknown Warrior of the First World War.

This circular route takes in three royal palaces, Westminster Abbey, the Houses of Parliament and St James's Park.

start / finish	Charing Cross Underground Station, Trafalgar Square exit (Bakerloo and Northern lines)
nearest postcode	WC2N 5DP
distance	2½ miles / 3.9 km
time	1 hour 30 minutes
terrain	Surfaced roads and paths; steps to descend; no steep hills.

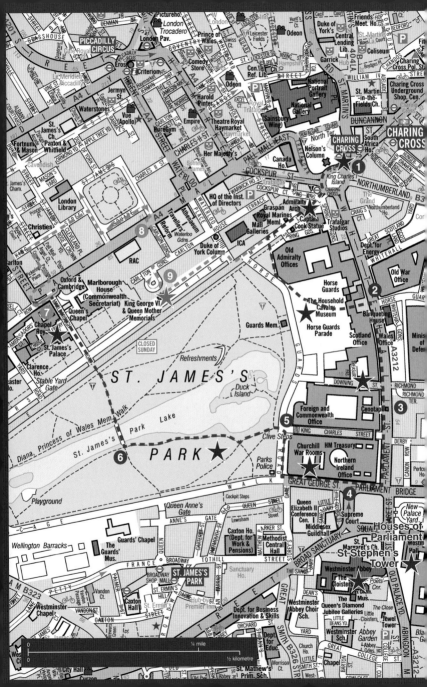

1 This circular tour starts at the Trafalgar Square exit from Charing Cross Station ★ . Walk along the south (Whitehall) side of the square and use the lights to cross to the far pavement of The Mall, an impressive red carpet to Buckingham Palace. Go through Admiralty Arch ★ , and, beyond the statue to Captain James Cook, bear left past the National Police Memorial into Horse Guards Parade ★ . Get here by 11.00 a.m., or 10 a.m. on Sunday (check online first), for a close view of the changing of a mounted guard protecting the long-gone Whitehall Palace. This is more spectacular and far less crowded than its Buckingham Palace counterpart.

2 Before going through the archway towards Whitehall, look up at the black mark on the clock by the number two. This marks the hour of King Charles I's beheading outside the first floor of the Banqueting House opposite, the last survivor of Whitehall Palace. Turn right along Whitehall. After the striking memorial to the women of the Second World War come the gates to Downing Street ★ , built by a political turncoat who spied on Oliver Cromwell for King Charles II while spying on the king for Cromwell. Number 10 is the official residence of the Prime Minister as First Lord of the Treasury.

3 Beyond the Cenotaph (empty tomb) which commemorates the country's war dead, turn right at the end of the road into Parliament Square. Across the square – behind the Church of St Margaret, Westminster, the parish church of the House of Commons – you will see Westminster Abbey ★ , and to its left lie the Houses of Parliament ★ and Westminster Hall. The nearer Elizabeth Tower houses the clock and its bell, Big Ben, while St Stephen's Tower ★ , which is over the main public entrance, was once the world's tallest building.

4 Continue into Great George Street, and turn right along Horse Guards Road. Past the Churchill War Rooms ★ , where the hotline to Washington masqueraded as Churchill's private lavatory, cross to St James's Park ★ .

5 Inside the park (acquired by King Henry VIII from St James's leper hospital), bear left along the lakeside. In the late 1600s the park housed pelicans, a crocodile and an elephant supplied with buckets of wine to keep out the cold. Only the pelicans remain.

6 Take the bridge on your right and pause halfway for a splendid vista left to Buckingham Palace and right to Horse Guards. Continue to the gate (public toilets here), cross The Mall and take Marlborough Road to St James's Palace ★ on the left. Foreign ambassadors to the UK are still accredited to the Court of St James.

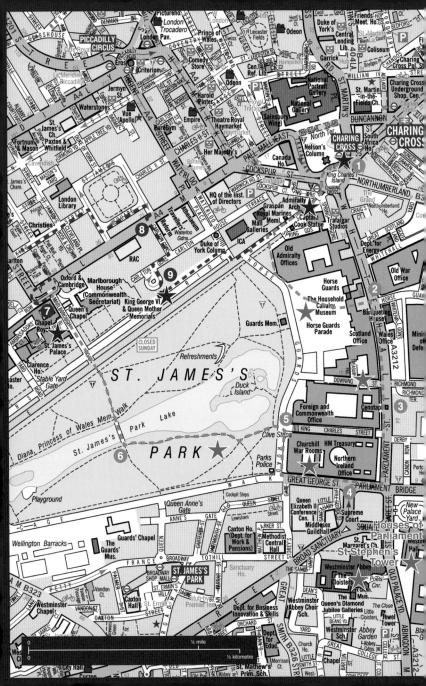

7 From the Palace, cross to the bottom of St James's Street (ahead of you to the left), go right along Pall Mall and left under the building arch into Crown Passage. The Red Lion pub is worth a visit. At King Street, turn right and pass Christie's to enter St James's Square. Here, turn right and then left to General Eisenhower's wartime headquarters, where a right turn takes you back into Pall Mall.

8 Take the zebra crossing into Carlton Gardens, which you follow right and then left to the King George VI Memorial ★. Down the steps and facing The Mall is the affectionate memorial to his wife, Queen Elizabeth The Queen Mother.

9 Go left along Horse Ride and rejoin The Mall by the Duke of York Steps. Continue to Admiralty Arch. All the statuary here has a naval connection, except for the plaster nose on a column halfway across the road. This was installed secretly by an artist protesting at the spread of CCTV cameras across the capital, but the mounted guardsmen have christened it 'Old Nosey' after the Duke of Wellington, and every new recruit has to touch it on their first ride through the arch! Retrace your steps to Trafalgar Square, where this walk ends.

ᴀᴢ walk thirteen

London's Villages: Soho

The West End's lively neighbour.

Soho was farmland until 1536, when King Henry VIII seized land from Abingdon Abbey and St Giles's Hospital for a hunting park. The name Soho originated from a hunting call, *So-ho!* As London expanded westward after the Great Fire of 1666, developers saw the area's potential; Golden Square was laid out by 1673, Gerrard Street and Soho Square in 1677. After Soho's aristocratic residents migrated to Mayfair in the mid-1700s, the area faced swift decline, attracting poor refugees and immigrants: French Protestants, Greeks, Italians and Russian and Polish Jews. Soho's cosmopolitan and bohemian air soon brought in writers, musicians, artists, revolutionaries and thinkers.

In the 1800s, Soho was famous for brothels, theatres, night clubs, and international dining, and in the 20th century, film and music companies moved into the area.

Gambling and the sex trade brought organized crime to Soho after the Second World War, and although these are no longer prominent, today the area retains a raffish reputation as an invigorating place for all kinds of entertainment. It also has the largest Chinatown in Europe.

This walk brings together the contrasting elements of this vibrant district.

start	Oxford Circus Underground Station (Bakerloo, Central and Victoria lines)
nearest postcode	W1B 3AG
finish	Tottenham Court Road Underground Station (Central and Northern lines)
distance	1½ miles / 2.4 km
time	45 minutes
terrain	Surfaced roads and paths; no steep hills.

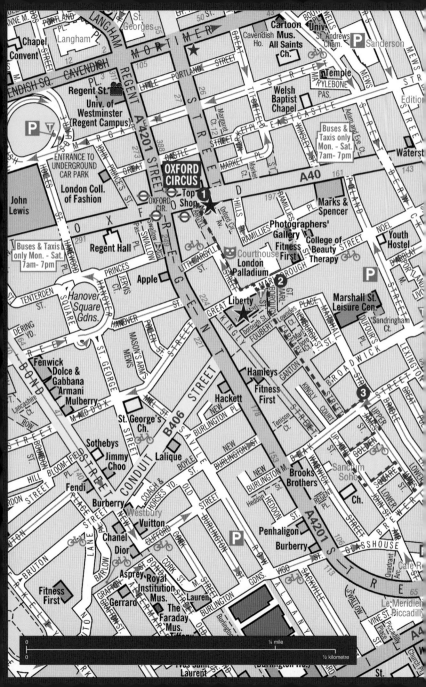

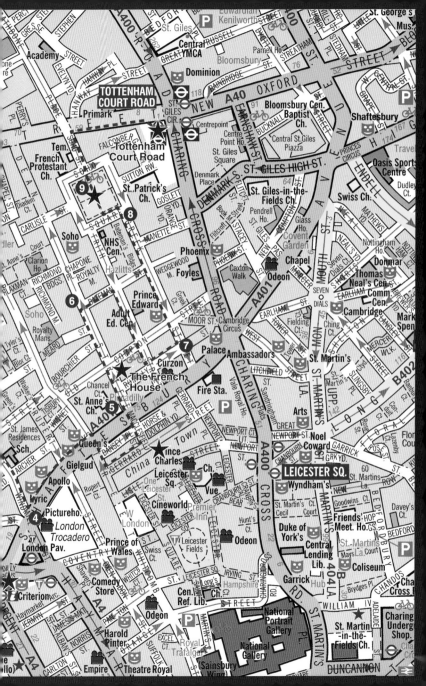

1 Leaving Oxford Circus Station ★ by the Argyll Street exit, dip into The Argyll Arms opposite, which has the best pub glasswork in London, before heading away from Oxford Street. Passing the 1910 London Palladium, go left to cross Great Marlborough Street to Liberty's ★. The store was opened in 1875 by Arthur Lasenby Liberty as East India House, selling oriental patterned silks and Japanese work, and the present extravaganza of a building, which includes timbers from two wooden warships, dates from 1925.

2 Left of Liberty's, bear right into Carnaby Street, famous in the 1960s for its fashion boutiques. As you pass Broadwick Street, where poet William Blake was born and where Dr John Snow discovered that cholera was spread through contaminated drinking water, pause to see how many you can recognize of the Soho luminaries in the mural there, before continuing to Beak Street, where you turn left. Italian painter Canaletto lodged here in the mid-1700s, and The Old Coffee House, once a temperance pub, is worth a visit.

3 Turn right along Upper James Street into Golden Square, whose 'mournful statue' nobody can identify with certainty. Go right, left and left again round the square, before turning right down Lower James Street. Turn left into Brewer Street by The Crown (once the Hickford Rooms where Mozart played). At Great Windmill Street, turn right past the remains of the Windmill Theatre to Shaftesbury Avenue.

4 Look right to the aluminium Angel of Christian Charity (popularly known as Eros ★) before heading left to Wardour Street, where you cross Shaftesbury Avenue to enter Chinatown ★. Go left along Gerrard Street and left again up Macclesfield Street to cross into Dean Street, where Karl Marx lived in 'an old hovel'.

5 In Dean Street is The French House ★ , formerly known as The York Minster and run from 1914 by the flamboyantly moustached Victor Berlemont and his son. It became a magnet for bohemian artists, and Dylan Thomas famously left the only manuscript of *Under Milk Wood* under a bench here during a pub crawl. At the corner with Old Compton Street, look left to The Admiral Duncan, the gay pub bombed in 1999 by a right-wing terrorist. Continue up Dean Street to Groucho's (45) and Duck Soup (41). As The Colony Room, Duck Soup was run by the notoriously foul-mouthed Muriel Belcher, who was famous for her put-downs and attracted some of the great names in British art to join the club when she ran it from 1948 to 1979.

6 Turn right along Bateman Street to The Dog and Duck, whose name recalls Soho's past as a hunting ground, and go right down Frith Street, past Ronnie Scott's Jazz Club (46) and the blue plaques to Mozart and the television pioneer John Logie Baird, to turn left along Romilly Street. Norman's was formerly The Coach and Horses, whose landlord was the notoriously rude Norman Balon, and whose clientele included Francis Bacon and Jeffrey Bernard.

7 Next, turn left up Greek Street, past L'Escargot (48), named by its first owner after his most famous dish. Georges Gaudin had a snail farm in the restaurant's cellar, and a plaster model on the façade shows him riding a huge snail, with the motto, 'Slow and Sure'.

8 Continue to Soho Square ★ . On the right-hand corner, at 1 Greek Street, is The House of St Barnabas, a charity for the homeless situated in a fine Georgian mansion. Spot the 'penny slide' for donations. Nearby is St Patrick's Church. The drag artist Danny La Rue was a choirboy here. Cross and turn left to enter Soho Square. By the mock-Tudor gardeners' storehouse in the centre, look left to the French Protestant Church, and right to number 14 where Mary Seacole, the great Jamaican Crimean War nurse, wrote her memoirs.

9 Passing King Charles II's statue, leave the square to cross to the right side of Soho Street. This leads to Oxford Street. A right turn takes you to Tottenham Court Road Station ★ where this walk ends opposite The Flying Horse, which has more good pub glass.

ᴬ̶Z̶ walk fourteen

Putting on the Ritz

High living and fine shopping in Piccadilly and
St James's.

In the early 1600s, Robert Baker, a Strand tailor, made a fortune by selling
picadils (fancy starched collars), and built a country house north of what is
now Piccadilly Circus. His house was soon nicknamed Piccadilly Hall. From
1660 onwards, the district began to attract the rich and the fashionable
who wanted to live close to the royal court. Great mansions sprang up along
the highway now known as Piccadilly, and Henry Jermyn, Earl of St Albans,
began to develop the area around St James's.

This circular walk takes in the houses of the wealthy and the upmarket
shops that served them, many of which display 'By Appointment' signs
proclaiming that they supply to the Royal Family. Many of the pubs
where the servants of wealthy households drank are still in business, and
the gentlemen's clubs of St James's, once notorious for the high-stakes
gambling that went on there, remain exclusive although much more
respectable. The route even includes a hotel that was in its time so luxurious
that it added a word to the English language: ritzy.

start / finish	Piccadilly Circus Underground Station
	(Bakerloo and Piccadilly lines)
nearest postcode	W1J 9HP
distance	2¾ miles / 4.5 km
time	1 hour 30 minutes
terrain	Surfaced roads and paths; no steep hills.

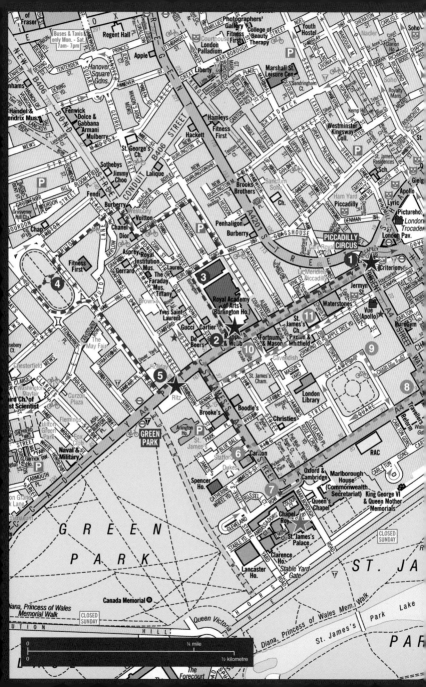

1 From the junction with Regent Street, by Exit 2 of Piccadilly Circus Underground Station, follow the north side of Piccadilly as far as Albany Courtyard. Since 1802, this has been a set of exclusive bachelor chambers for residents ranging from Lord Byron to Edward Heath. Next comes Burlington House ★. This last survivor of the great Piccadilly mansions of the 1660s now houses the Royal Academy.

2 After Burlington House, turn right into Burlington Arcade, first built to stop rubbish being thrown into Burlington House gardens. It is policed by beadles, who make up Britain's oldest and smallest private police force. They have been employed since the arcade opened in 1819 to keep the riffraff out of the arcade by 'preventing whistling, singing, carrying large parcels or open umbrellas and pushing perambulators'.

3 At the end of the arcade, turn right along Burlington Gardens. At Vigo Street, cross to Savile Row, a byword for high-quality bespoke tailoring. At New Clifford Street, turn left. Follow the street as it turns to the right, past the Dior store, and turn left into Bruton Street. Just past the plaque on the left marking the birthplace of Queen Elizabeth II, turn left into Berkeley Square.

4 Cross to the far side of the square. Number 44, now Annabelle's nightclub and The Claremont gambling club, was visited in 1986 by a 'policewoman' and a 'traffic warden' (in fact Princess Diana and Sarah Ferguson). Both were turned away for being in uniform. Go left, past number 45, where the colonial governor known as Clive of India took his own life in 1774, and number 50, once deemed the most haunted house in London, to follow the square left past Phillips auction house and turn right along Berkeley Street back to Piccadilly.

5 Turn left opposite the 'ritzy' Ritz Hotel ★, cross Piccadilly at the traffic lights, and walk down St James's Street. This is a street of gentlemen's clubs: Boodles; Brook's, where in the 1700s, 'a thousand meadows and cornfields were staked at every throw'; White's, where £3,000 was once bet on which of two raindrops would reach the bottom of the pane first; and the Carlton, where membership was limited to male Conservative Party members until 2009 and where Margaret Thatcher was admitted as an 'honorary man'.

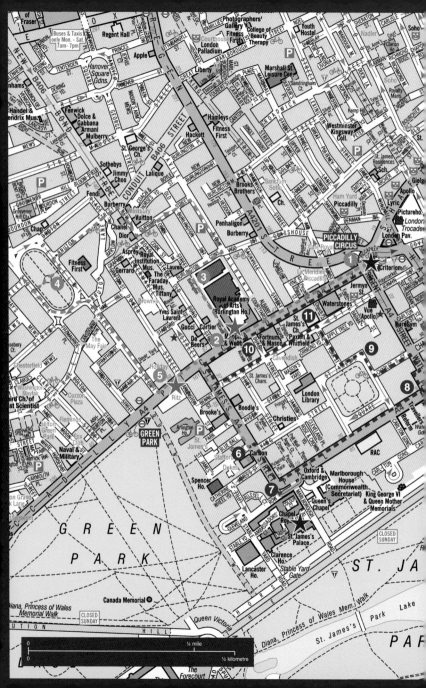

6 Cross the road and continue past King Street to a cluster of shops close to St James's Palace. Lobb's has sold handmade boots since 1850.

A couple of doors away, Lock's supplied hats to the Duke of Wellington and Admiral Nelson (Nelson's with a built-in eyepatch) and invented the billycock hat, or bowler, as suitable protective headgear for gamekeepers. A little further along, across Pickering Place (the smallest square in London) is Berry Brothers and Rudd, wine merchants to the Royal Family. Originally the Widow Bourne's grocer's shop, the establishment still has the coffee scales where generations of notables chose to be weighed, plus a record of their weights.

7 Opposite St James's Palace ★, turn left along Pall Mall. Across the road, past the Oxford and Cambridge Club, Nell Gwynne, King Charles II's mistress, lived at number 79. Schomberg House next door was once the Temple of Health and Hymen where, in the 1780s, couples wishing to conceive could occupy the electrically charged Grand Celestial State Bed for £50 per night.

8 Opposite the Athenaeum Club, turn left into Waterloo Place, and left again along Charles II Street into St James's Square. Turn right here. In the corner is the In and Out Club, once the residence of Nancy Astor, the first woman to take a seat in Parliament. Here, you can also pause at the

memorial to WPC Yvonne Fletcher, who was killed in 1984 by a gunshot fired from the Libyan People's Bureau, then at number 5.

9 Go left and then right along Duke of York Street, past the ornate Red Lion pub and Trumper's upmarket barber's shop, to the church of St James's Piccadilly, designed by Christopher Wren with carving by Grinling Gibbons. Left along Jermyn Street are more of the many specialist shops set up to supply the local great houses. Continue across Duke Street and past Beau Brummel's statue to turn right up St James's Street and right again along Piccadilly.

10 Return past Duke Street to Fortnum & Mason. Charles Fortnum, a footman to King George III, was responsible for refilling the royal candelabra. He sold the used candles and used the proceeds to open a luxury grocery store with his friend John Mason, who handled the deliveries. They feature on the clock.

11 Continue past Hatchards bookshop, founded in 1801 and now owned by Waterstones, whose flagship store occupies the former premises of Simpson's, the model for Grace Brothers in the popular sitcom *Are You Being Served?* Piccadilly Circus is at the end of the road, where this walk ends.

AZ walk fifteen

A Royal Route

Regent's Park to Trafalgar Square along London's
grand boulevard.

When the Prince of Wales (later King George IV) commissioned John Nash
to develop Regent's Park in the 1820s, he wanted to connect it with his city
centre residence at Carlton House by a grand boulevard rivalling those of
Paris.

This walk follows the route from the park along Portland Place, which was
designed by the Adams Brothers as a street of palaces. Although many of
these palaces are no longer standing, enough remains to make this still a
prestigious address, attracting embassies and international companies.
At the south end are the headquarters of the BBC, The Langham hotel
and Nash's church of All Souls Langham Place, which marks a curve to
the north end of Regent Street, a new thoroughfare driven through cheap
property on the western edge of rundown Soho and separating Soho from
the fashionable West End. Nash's New Street soon became the 'centre of
fashion', and it remains a shopping mecca.

From Piccadilly Circus our route runs down Haymarket and into Trafalgar
Square. This was cleared by Nash but not developed until the 1840s.
Fronting the 1837 National Gallery and St Martin-in-the-Fields, this grand
piazza is dominated by a column commemorating Horatio Nelson's naval
victories. The Prince Regent would have loved it!

start	Regent's Park Underground Station (Bakerloo line)
nearest postcode	NW1 5HA
finish	Charing Cross Underground Station
	(Bakerloo and Northern lines)
distance	2 miles / 3.1 km
time	1 hour
terrain	Surfaced roads and paths; no steep hills.

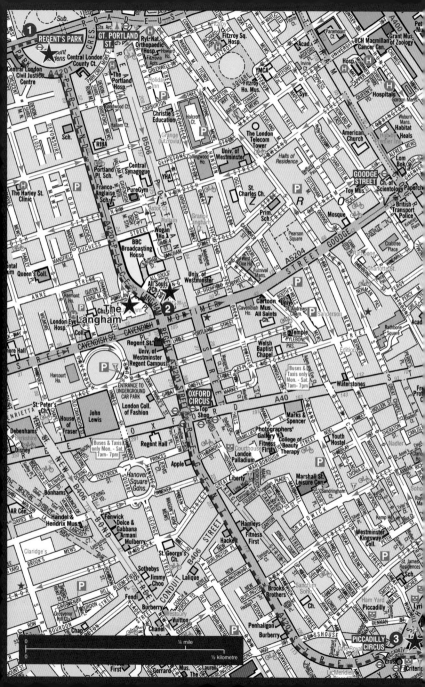

1 From Regent's Park Station ★ , turn left, cross Park Crescent, and follow it left to Portland Place, where you turn right. Between Weymouth Street and New Cavendish Street, numbers 27–47 give a sense of how the street once looked, and across the road, numbers 46–48 make an eye-catching survivor. Ahead, bear left to pass the massive Italianate Langham hotel ★ . The Langham was one of the first of London's grand hotels and supremely luxurious. Bombed in the 1940 Blitz, it was for a while used by the BBC, but reopened as the Langham Hilton in 1991. Opposite is the BBC's Broadcasting House. At the brilliantly original All Souls Langham Place ★ , the road bends right to Oxford Circus.

2 Regent Street begins after All Souls. Continue past the University of Westminster, formerly a polytechnic where in 1964 a group of students formed the rock band Pink Floyd. Cross straight over at the lights to remain on Regent Street. Some of the big stores have gone, but Liberty, Hamleys and the Café Royal remain on the left-hand side, and the street still specializes in high-end fashion goods.

3 At Piccadilly Circus ★ , where Regent Street meets Piccadilly, cross diagonally to the Criterion restaurant and theatre. The 1893 aluminium statue we know as Eros commemorates the philanthropic Earl of Shaftesbury and was intended to represent the Angel of Christian Charity. It was positioned so that its arrow (shaft) when fired would end up buried in Shaftesbury Avenue opposite. (The Victorians did love their puns!)

4 Turn right down Haymarket, which really was once a market for hay and straw. It became notorious in the 1800s as 'the great parade ground of abandoned women'. One exquisite 18th-century shop remains at number 34. Nowadays, Haymarket is best known for its theatres and cinema. The Theatre Royal Haymarket ★ dates from 1720 and the present building, reputedly haunted, is the work of John Nash. At the Charles II Street lights, cross left to the Theatre Royal and continue down Haymarket past Her Majesty's Theatre on the right.

5 At the foot of Haymarket, go left and take Pall Mall East into the pedestrianized area of Trafalgar Square.

6 The square began to be laid out in 1840 by Sir Charles Barry in front of the National Gallery, which holds a collection of artworks dating from the 13th to the early 20th century. Its 1991 Sainsbury Wing appalled Prince Charles, who called it 'a monstrous carbuncle', but it has enabled the gallery to expand its display significantly. Beyond is the church of St Martin-in-the-Fields. The present building dates from the 1720s and was designed by James Gibb. Buckingham Palace lies in its parish, it displays the royal arms above its entrance, and Charles II was baptized here.
St Martin's is famous for its concerts and for its work with young people and the homeless. It holds services for the local Chinese community, and has a crypt café which you might like to try at the end of this walk.
The most prominent feature of Trafalgar Square is the 169-foot (51-metre) high Nelson's Column, erected in 1843. The plaques around the base highlight Nelson's most famous naval victories and are made of metal melted down

from captured French cannon. The four bronze lions by Landseer were added in 1867. He had the corpse of a lion delivered to his studio and took so long over his task that neighbours complained about the stench!
The statues in the square are largely military, naval and royal, but George Washington stands outside the National Gallery on imported American soil, and the empty fourth plinth hosts modern sculptures in rotation, each one staying for 12–18 months. The fountains come into their own at times of celebration, and the square, which looks directly down towards the Houses of Parliament, is also a focus for political meetings and demonstrations.

7 From the northeast corner of the square, opposite St Martin-in-the-Fields, walk down towards Whitehall, with South Africa House on your left. At the foot of the square, look far right to Admiralty Arch and Canada House before arriving at the entrance to Charing Cross Underground Station ★, where the walk ends. Just before the station is a stone pillar with windows and a door. This used to be the smallest police station in Britain. Don't miss it.

A·Z walk sixteen

Luxurious London

Affluence and espionage in Mayfair.

Ironically, one of London's most exclusive districts is named after an annual May fair once described as 'a disgrace to the Creation'. The fair lasted about a fortnight, with attractions ranging from bare-knuckle fighting to semolina-eating contests. Originally sited close to St James's Palace, it was soon moved to an area of marshy fields of very little value, left by law-writer and moneylender Hugh Audley to his great-niece, Mary Davies.

In 1677, aged 12, Mary married Sir Thomas Grosvenor, at a time when fashionable Londoners were moving west. By 1720, Mary Davies's grandson, Sir Richard Grosvenor, had designed a grid pattern of new streets, with a large square at its centre. Five years later, Daniel Defoe recorded 'an amazing Scene of new Foundations, not of Houses only, but as I may say of New Cities, New Squares and fine Buildings…' Needless to say, this new development close to the royal court was far too grand for the fair, which was moved on again to the East End and then suppressed.

Mayfair became a magnet for the wealthy and fashionable, with all they could require for their comfort. It soon eclipsed earlier fashionable districts like Soho and Covent Garden, and its fortunes have never declined, a reflection of its value on the Monopoly™ board!

start / finish	Bond Street Underground Station (Central and Jubilee lines)
nearest postcode	W1R 1FE
distance	2 miles / 3.4 km
time	1 hour
terrain	Surfaced roads and paths; steps to climb and descend; no steep hills.

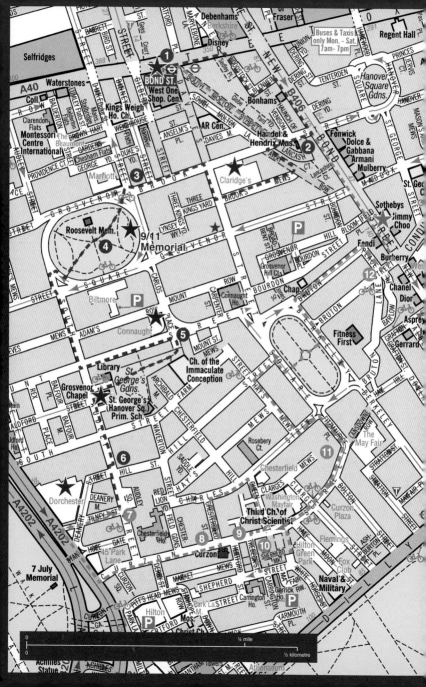

① Take the Oxford Street exit from Bond Street Station ★. Turn right and cross Davies Street and South Molton Street. At Woodstock Street, go right, bear left at the end along Blenheim Street, and turn right into New Bond Street, passing Bonham's Auction House and several art galleries where you may want to browse.

② At Brook Street, cross to the far pavement and turn right past the former houses of Handel and Jimi Hendrix. Go left into Avery Row and right by The Iron Duke pub along Brook's Mews, one of many where wealthy residents originally kept their horses and carriages. Facing Three Kings Yard, turn right into Davies Street. At Claridge's hotel ★, a byword for luxury since its foundation by a butler in 1856. Cross Brook Street and turn right to follow it round to Grosvenor Square.

③ Here, cross over to see the house on the corner of Duke Street, where the second US president John Adams lived during a diplomatic mission to Britain in the 1780s. Follow the zebra crossings into the square. A board by the gate summarizes its history and describes its main features. It is worth visiting the understated 9/11 memorial ★ nearby.

④ Cross the square diagonally towards the site of the old US Embassy; until the US Embassy moved to Battersea, this was the only US embassy building not owned by the US Government but rented (from the Duke of Westminster). Take the crossing left into South Audley Street. On the corner of Mount Street, James Purdey and Sons have been making sporting guns for 200 years; Queen Victoria granted the firm a royal warrant in 1838. Turn left to follow Mount Street past more high-end shops and restaurants to the Connaught Hotel ★.

⑤ Here, loop right through the gardens; there are helpful information boards. Passing the Church of the Immaculate Conception, re-enter South Audley Street by Grosvenor Chapel ★. This was used by US forces during the Second World War. Cross to Thomas Goode's china shop to look back at the chapel, and continue to the far end of the shop to admire the dazzling tilework.

⑥ At Hill Street traffic lights, cross South Audley Street and continue on to Audley Square, where Soviet agents exchanged chalked messages on the lamppost close to EON Productions, makers of the James Bond film *Dr. No*.

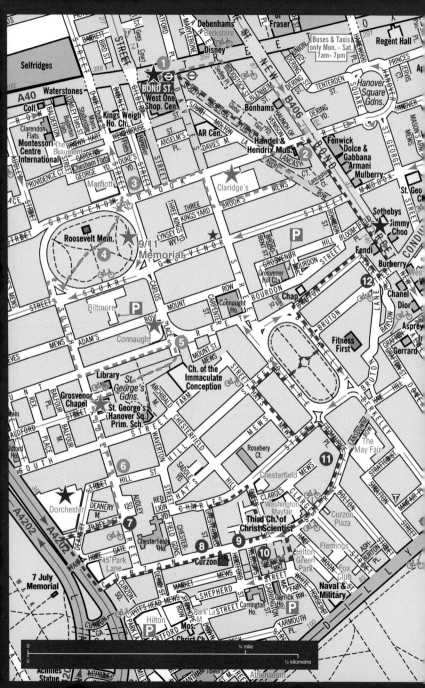

7 Turn right along Tilney Street to reach the Dorchester hotel ★, home in the war years to General Eisenhower, before bearing left down Park Lane across Stanhope Gate and left into Curzon Street, a mecca of gambling, where private gaming clubs rub shoulders with high-street bookmakers.

8 Past Crockfords casino, go left along Chesterfield Street. Three former prime ministers lived around here: Anthony Eden in number 4, Benjamin Disraeli back in 19 Curzon Street, and Lord Rosebery around the corner in 20 Charles Street. Turn right into Charles Street and right again. At the end of Queen Street, take the double crossing to go right along Curzon Street.

9 Opposite is Crewe House, now the Saudi Arabian Embassy. It was built in 1730 by Edward Shepherd, the architect who planned the district. Turn left down Hertford Street, home to George Cayley, the first successful designer of heavier-than-air flying machines, left into Shepherd Street and right up Trebeck Street with its May Fair plaque.

10 Go right into Shepherd Market. On the left, in a small square under a tree is number 50a, a discreet brothel licensed by Westminster Council on the grounds of 'long-established usage'. Continue to Ye Grapes pub and go left up the alleyway to cross Curzon Street and turn right.

11 After Trumper's matchless barber's shop and the Christian Science Centre, bear left towards Berkeley Square along Fitzmaurice Place and take the double zebra crossing back into Charles Street. At The Footman pub, go right along Hays Mews and right again by The Coach and Horses into Hill Street. Take the zebra crossing to Berkeley Square, and walk across the square to the far side. Go left, take the double zebra crossing across Bruton Street, and go right along quiet Bruton Place.

12 Emerging into Bruton Street, turn left, and left again up New Bond Street, with Sotheby's auctioneers ★ on the right. Across Grosvenor Street, continue to Fenwick's department store and turn left along Brook Street. Past Haunch of Venison Yard, go diagonally right up South Molton Street to Oxford Street and then left across Davies Street to Bond Street Station.

AZ walk seventeen

London's Villages: Chelsea

The fashionable home of royalty and rock stars.

Just as the origin of its name is disputed (Chalk Wharf, Shelf of Sand, Gravel Bank), so Chelsea has had frequent changes of image. It started as a riverside fishing village. By the 16th century it was the Village of Palaces, where Thomas More and King Henry VIII had country mansions. The next two centuries brought Christopher Wren's Royal Hospital (a home for former soldiers), Chelsea Physic Garden, and the fashionable pleasure gardens of Ranelagh. In the 19th and early 20th centuries, Chelsea attracted writers and painters, both successful and struggling, until in the Swinging Sixties it emerged as a magnet for rock stars, fashionistas and avant-garde artists.

This circular walk begins at Sloane Square, named after Sir Hans Sloane, a royal physician, who was Lord of the Manor of Chelsea in the 1700s. From there, the route follows the King's Road. Originally a guarded private road used by Charles II to reach Hampton Court, it is now a fashionable shopping street.

The walk goes on to the Royal Hospital and the site of Ranelagh Gardens, and meets the river at Chelsea Physic Garden. At Chelsea Old Church, it turns inland towards the Old Town Hall, scene of many notable weddings, and returns to Sloane Square along King's Road.

start / finish	Sloane Square Underground Station (Circle and District lines)
nearest postcode	SW1W 8BB
distance	3 miles / 4.8 km
time	1 hour 30 minutes
terrain	Surfaced roads and paths; no steep hills.

1 From Sloane Square Station ★, carefully cross the road straight ahead of you, to the south side of Sloane Square. Continue across Lower Sloane Street to enter King's Road. A narrow left-hand turning leads into Duke of York Square. Once in the square, go right and look out for the plan of Charles II's private road, set into the paving.

2 Returning right to King's Road, turn left down Cheltenham Terrace and Franklin's Row, with the old barracks, now Saatchi Gallery ★, on your left. At Royal Hospital Road, cross. Turn right to pass the Royal Hospital ★ and the National Army Museum ★, and go left down Tite Street, where Oscar Wilde and the artist Whistler, rival wits, once lived ('I went past your house this afternoon,' said Whistler. 'Thank you,' replied Wilde).

3 At the end of Tite Street, opposite the Peace Pagoda across the Thames, go right along Chelsea Embankment, crossing Swan Walk, to the river wall of Chelsea Physic Garden ★, established in 1673 to grow medicinal plants. Its location enabled explorers and collectors to unload their finds straight from the river.

4 Continuing to Royal Hospital Road, cross at the lights, go sharp right past the gardens, and turn left along Cheyne Walk, full of blue plaques to notable residents from Lloyd George (10) to Rossetti (16), whose garden menagerie included a pelican, a wallaby, and a wombat which ate a lady's hat. A plaque on the entrance to Cheyne Mews marks the site of Henry VIII's grand country retreat. More amusing is the notice further down on the left.

5 Cross Oakley Street and continue along Cheyne Walk where Mick Jagger lived for ten years at number 48. Cheyne Row on the right leads to the house of the Victorian literary couple, Thomas and Jane Carlyle. Carlyle was attracted by the cheapness of the 'roomy and sufficient' house, but found the noise unbearable and soundproofed his study with cork. On the corner, the chastely decorated Carlyle Mansions have housed the unlikely combination of writers Henry James, T. S. Eliot and Ian Fleming.

6 Chelsea Old Church ahead is where Thomas More, Lord Chancellor to Henry VIII, worshipped. His Beaufort House stood nearby, and his statue faces the Thames. The ornate lamppost nearby commemorates the building of the Chelsea Embankment.

7 Further along the Embankment is Crosby Moran Hall ★ , a 15th-century mansion once occupied by King Richard III and later owned by Thomas More. Originally named Crosby Hall, it was relocated here from Bishopsgate in 1910 and is now a private residence. The current owner is rumoured to have spent £50 million lavishly restoring it.

8 Retrace your steps to Old Church Street and turn left. Notice the tile pictures on 46a, originally a dairy, and the pub name which reminds us of the nearby site of Chelsea's famous pottery. Charles Kingsley, the 19th-century author of *The Water Babies*, lived in the Old Rectory at the top of the street, whose garden claims to be the second largest in Central London after Buckingham Palace.

9 Turn right along King's Road. Just before Oakley Street, cross towards the fire station with its board of honour, turn left up Dovehouse Street and right along Britten Street into Sydney Street. Turn right south of the vast St Luke's Church ★ , where Charles Dickens married Catherine Hogarth, to rejoin King's Road opposite Chelsea Old Town Hall.

10 Turn left, past The Pheasantry (152), a pizza restaurant with a colourful history. Mary Quant began her career at 138a, and Thomas Crapper's lavatory showroom occupied 120. Opposite, on the corner of Royal Avenue, was the Chelsea Drugstore.

11 At the end of King's Road, loop left, crossing Symons Street to go right along Sloane Square and cross Sloane Street to the magnificent Holy Trinity Church ★ , described by John Betjeman as the 'Cathedral of the Arts and Crafts Movement'.

12 After Holy Trinity, turn right into Sloane Terrace. Opposite Cadogan Hall, originally a Christian Scientist church, turn right down Sedding Street and cross to the Royal Court Theatre, birthplace of 'kitchen sink' drama. The walk ends at Sloane Square Station.

AZ walk eighteen

A Park Fit for a Prince

A stroll around Regent's Park.

This circular walk explores the finest of London's Royal Parks. Regent's Park was formerly a royal hunting ground, whose transformation was in part a vanity project and in part an inspired piece of town planning on a grand scale.

The scheme, sponsored by the Prince Regent (later King George IV) in the 1820s and largely carried out by John Nash and his protégé Decimus Burton, was to provide income for the crown and beautify the capital. The picturesque landscaping imitated the informal parkland of great English country houses, and the development was surrounded by palatial-looking terraces divided into several separate residences. The exclusive suburb was to be connected to Westminster by a splendid new avenue, and, to add an exotic touch, London Zoo was situated to the north.

Under pressure from Parliament, the Prince Regent gradually opened his park to the public, and, as more urban parks were created for public recreation, Regent's Park became an influential model, not only in Britain but across the world. The fairytale villas and terraces remain exclusive, but the Prince's great park is ours to enjoy.

This walk may be combined with walk 15 for a longer tour of Regency London. Follow the directions at step 6.

start / finish	Baker Street Underground Station (Bakerloo, Circle, Hammersmith & City, Jubilee and Metropolitan lines)
nearest postcode	NW1 5LJ
distance	3¼ miles / 5.1 km (5½ miles / 8.7 km if combined with walk 15)
time	1 hour 45 minutes (2 hours 45 minutes if combined with walk 15)
terrain	Surfaced roads and paths; no steep hills.

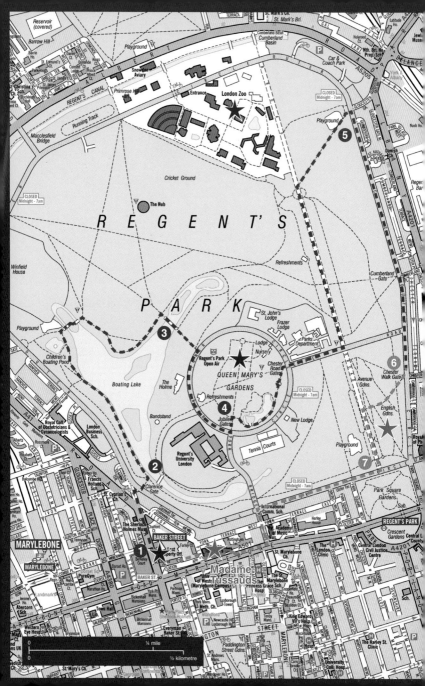

1 Take the Baker Street (North) exit from the station ★ and turn right. Abbey House on the left stands on the site of 221B Baker Street, Sherlock Holmes's fictional residence, and there are echoes of the great detective along the street, including a Sherlock Holmes Museum. Cross Allsop Place at the traffic lights and continue to the end of Baker Street, going round to the right to cross Cornwall Terrace (the first of Regent's Park's great terraces) and entering the park by Clarence Gate.

2 Turn left along the lake, which is fed by the River Tyburn. Past the island is a view right to The Holme, one of Nash's splendid villas, while to the left are glimpses of the surprising domes of Sussex Place. Bear right towards the café and boat hire office, with the minaret of London Central Mosque in view half-left. Go right over the blue bridges, and keep right, skirting the lake. Throughout the walk, keep your eyes open for information boards indicating interesting features of the park, such as the many species of resident and seasonal birds.

3 Reaching the stone Longbridge, cross right and continue to Inner Circle. Here, turn right. Just past Regent's University, at the junction with York Bridge, cross left to Jubilee Gates and enter Queen Mary's Gardens ★. Take the path to the right with the lake on your left. Queen Mary (George V's wife) loved roses, and her rose garden continues to the Chester Road Gates.

4 Cross Inner Circle and take the left pavement of Chester Road as far as a gate, where you turn left into the park. Follow Broad Walk past two of many cafés along the route until you reach the odd Ready Money Drinking Fountain. (Here is a chance to break your journey by continuing straight to London Zoo ★ and rejoining the walk after your visit.) Go diagonally right, past the playground, to leave by Gloucester Gate.

5 Turn right along Outer Circle. You may notice that the bases of the lamp-posts commemorate the monarchs closely identified with the park: George IV, William IV and Elizabeth II. On your left, after Gloucester Gate, you pass the flamboyant Cumberland Terrace. This was planned to complement a small palace opposite, which was never built, and it is surmounted by statues highlighting Britain's achievements. Next comes Chester Terrace, the longest of the Nash terraces. Crossing Chester Road, continue to the end of the terrace and turn right to re-enter the park.

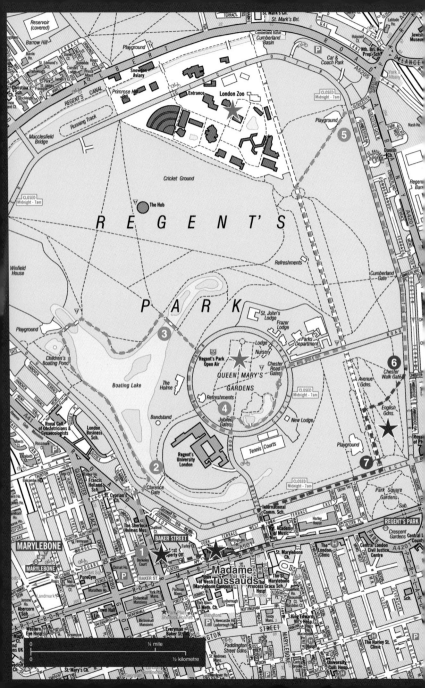

6 Go diagonally left, and loop right, into the English Gardens ★ , where you follow the central avenue left to leave the park and turn right along Outer Circle. (If you fancy a longer walk, you can cross the road and turn left along Park Square West, cross Marylebone Road at the traffic lights, and follow Walk 15 from Park Crescent opposite.)

7 Continue right along Outer Circle past Ulster Terrace. At the traffic lights, turn left along York Gate towards Marylebone Church. Then go right, passing Madame Tussauds ★ and the Planetarium. Across Allsop Place, the Sherlock Holmes statue marks Baker Street Station entrance.

AZ walk nineteen

Royal Kensington

Between Notting Hill and Albertopolis.

Kensington as we know it owes its existence to a king's asthma. Until the late 17th century, the area was little more than woodland and open heath, with a few market gardens and a couple of country houses. Then, in 1689, King William III found his lungs unable to withstand the smoke of Whitehall and bought Nottingham House, which he and Queen Mary II developed into their winter palace of Kensington. Since then, its residents have included Queen Victoria, who was born here, Prince Charles and Princess Diana, and the Duke and Duchess of Cambridge.

Although the new palace attracted some development to the area, large-scale expansion did not occur until the time of the Great Exhibition of 1851. This was a showcase of British science, arts and manufacture, spearheaded by Prince Albert, the Prince Consort, who is memorialized in the Albert Memorial and the Royal Albert Hall. The legacy of this exhibition can be found in the museum district popularly known as Albertopolis.

Kensington remains a fashionable residential area whose park, museums, shops and royal connections are all covered in this walk. On a Saturday, this walk could be combined with a visit to Portobello Market, signposted from Pembridge Road north of Notting Hill Gate Underground Station.

start	Notting Hill Gate Underground Station (Central, Circle and District lines)
nearest postcode	W11 3HT
finish	South Kensington Underground Station (District, Circle and Piccadilly lines)
distance	2¾ miles / 4.5 km
time	1 hour 30 minutes
terrain	Surfaced roads and paths; steps to descend; no steep hills.

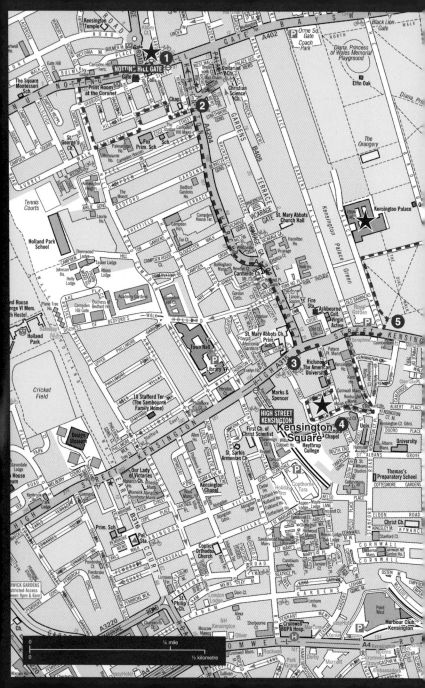

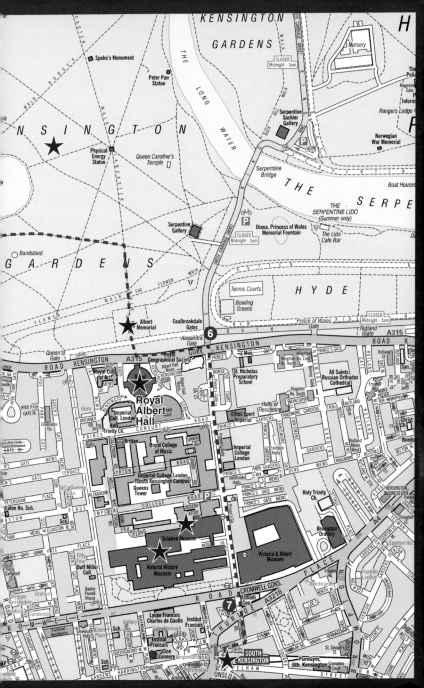

❶ Taking the south exit from Notting Hill Gate Station ★ , turn right, passing the Gate Picturehouse and the Coronet Theatre on your left. At Campden Hill Road, turn left, crossing Uxbridge Street, and left again at Kensington Place to enter a quiet neighbourhood of pastel-painted houses. Go left again into Hillgate Street, right into Hillgate Place and right along Jameson Street with its rooftop gardens. At the end of Jameson Street, rejoin Kensington Place, going left towards Kensington Church Street.

❷ Turn right into Kensington Church Street and follow it to the end. This opulent street, full of antique shops and estate agents' offices, confirms the wealth of the area. At the foot of Church Street, pause to look at the imposing Gothic Revival St Mary Abbots Church with its 278-foot (85-metre) tower and spire. Across the road, the stores of Kensington High Street, which once rivalled Oxford Street, have moved with the times. In the Sixties, Biba took over Derry & Toms near the Underground station. Now, most of the High Street is given over to food, with the entire Barker's building occupied by Whole Foods' vast range of organic, ethically sourced goods.

❸ Cross the High Street at the traffic lights, go left, and at Young Street turn right. Passing the novelist William Makepeace Thackeray's imposing house, continue to Kensington Square ★ . Turn right to follow three sides of the square in an anticlockwise direction. This was where residential Kensington started, and the blue plaques around it are proof of its continuing appeal; notice the door-hood of number 11.

❹ Continue into Thackeray Street with its surprisingly ordinary corner shop, and turn left to walk up Kensington Court, continuing straight ahead at the first corner and along the alleyway in front of Palace Place Mansions to join Kensington Road. Turn right towards the Royal Garden Hotel. Opposite, Kensington Palace Gardens (aka 'Millionaires' Row') is one of the world's most expensive and exclusive streets, home to eight embassies. Continue past the Goat Tavern, a pub since 1702, and cross over at the pedestrian crossing. Then go left to enter Kensington Gardens ★ .

5 Follow the path diagonally right, and then go left along the wall. At the railings, turn right along the front of Kensington Palace ★ ; through the gates is a statue of William III. Keep on across the Princess Diana Memorial Walk with the Round Pond on your left. Take the second path to your right, where you will see ahead the elaborate Albert Memorial ★ , with the Royal Albert Hall ★ behind it. After viewing the memorial, descend two sets of steps and turn left along the roadway.

6 At Alexandra Gate, cross over at the traffic lights and turn right to walk down Exhibition Road; the roads from the right have few controlled crossings, so take care. Passing Imperial College and the Science Museum on the right and the Victoria and Albert Museum on the left, cross straight over Cromwell Road. Looking back, you see on your left Alfred Waterhouse's fabulously ornate Natural History Museum, which attracts more than five million visitors a year, and on your right the Victoria and Albert (the V&A), Britain's foremost museum of fine and applied arts.

7 Continue on Exhibition Road and across Thurloe Place, then turn right along Thurloe Street to South Kensington Station ★ , where the walk ends.

AZ walk twenty

Where East Meets West

A walk through the Royal Borough of Greenwich.

Greenwich, the 'green port' of the Anglo-Saxons, was an insignificant fishing village on the River Thames until King Henry V's brother enclosed Greenwich Park in the 1420s for deer hunting and built Bella Court, which became Greenwich Palace. King Henry VIII and his daughters, Mary Tudor and Elizabeth I, were all born here.

In the 1670s, Christopher Wren built the Royal Observatory in Greenwich Park, away from the smoky skies of Central London. The Prime Meridian (0 degrees longitude) was established here in 1851, which means that you can stand with one foot in the east and one in the west.

The town's connections with the sea began when Henry VIII established a royal dockyard in neighbouring Deptford, and a hospital for disabled seamen was built here. In 1873 this became the Royal Naval College, closing in 1997, the same year that Maritime Greenwich was designated a UNESCO World Heritage Site.

This circular walk visits the Old Royal Naval College and runs through the heart of the town before making a circuit of the picturesque park, passing the Observatory which is now a museum. It includes a riverside walk and a breathtaking panorama of Central London. Its last stop is Greenwich Market, best visited at the weekend. There are plenty of places to stop for refreshments along the way.

start / finish	Cutty Sark Station (Docklands Light Railway)
nearest postcode	SE10 9SW
distance	4¼ miles / 6.9 km
time	2 hours 15 minutes
terrain	Surfaced roads and paths; steps to climb; one very steep hill.

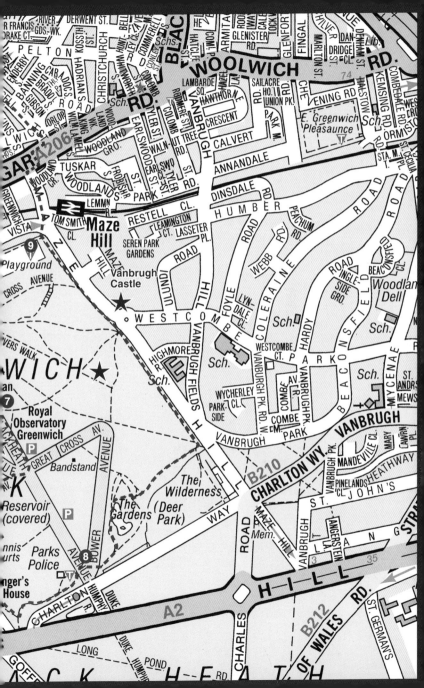

❶ Leaving Cutty Sark Station ★, take the alleyway left to Greenwich Church Street, turning left towards the Cutty Sark and continuing as far as her figurehead at the far end. Turn right here. Entering the gardens by the Visitor Centre, walk along the Thames frontage of the Old Royal Naval College ★ (now Greenwich University).

❷ Reaching Grand Square, turn right, looking uphill to the Royal Observatory Museum and Planetarium. Walk on to face on your left Queen Mary Court with its fine chapel and on your right King William Court with its magnificent Painted Hall. Knowledge of time and wind was vital to sailors, and the clock and wind dial on these buildings were meant to be seen from the river. For a further visible time check, the red ball above the Observatory was dropped every day at exactly 1.00 p.m.

❸ Turn right towards the gate, and at the end, go left along King William Walk. At the junction, go a few yards left to cross Romney Road; then turn right across King William Walk, and continue along Nelson Road to bear left into Greenwich High Road. Opposite, St Alfege Church stands where Archbishop Alfege was murdered in 1012 by his Viking kidnappers after refusing to be ransomed. Henry VIII was christened here.

❹ Take the zebra crossing across Stockwell Street and turn left up here, then right along Burney Street. Opposite the old Town Hall, go left along Royal Hill. Turn left by the postbox, and follow the right side of the often-filmed Gloucester Circus to Croom's Hill. Crossing the road, go left downhill, and, passing Greenwich Theatre, turn right by the Spread Eagle, formerly a coaching inn.

❺ At the end of Nevada Street, enter Greenwich Park ★ and go left along the rear of the National Maritime Museum ★. Past the huge ship in a bottle, turn left and climb the steps. Cross the colonnade and descend to the path bordering the museum. Take the first right to take in Inigo Jones's Queen's House. Then continue to Park Row to re-enter the park by the gate in the wall.

❻ Walk diagonally right towards the clump of trees at the foot of the hill. Turn left and climb the steep path to the Observatory ★ and the Prime Meridian Line. Below James Wolfe's statue is a spectacular view over London; a plaque indicates what you can see. Until 1857, this would have included the riotous Greenwich Fair. A popular entertainment, indecorous and occasionally lethal, was 'tumbling' down the hill.

7 With the Observatory on your right, follow Blackheath Avenue. Past the Tea House, go right to cross The Avenue (beware bicycles!) and take Great Cross Avenue, bordered by Anglo-Saxon tumuli, to Croomshill Gate. Turn left along Conduit Avenue and through the Rose Garden, passing the Ranger's House. Reaching the wall at the top of the park, turn left through The Dell to cross Blackheath Avenue just past the public toilets.

8 Take the gate leading to the Flower Garden, bear left to the lake, and follow its west shore. Curve right at the north end. Continue across the first path on the right. At the second, turn right and then left through The Gardens to reach the park wall. Here, turn left beside the wall to descend. On the right, you will glimpse the extraordinary 'Castle': a folly built by architect John Vanbrugh in 1719 and supposedly based on the Bastille where he had been imprisoned.

9 At the foot of the hill, leave the park to turn right along Park Vista and left down Maze Hill. Cross right at the traffic lights and then left again across Trafalgar Road. Go right to reach Lassell Street, where you turn left. Continue across Old Woolwich Road to Ballast Quay with views of the O2 Arena downriver. Turn left to follow the Thames past Greenwich Power Station, now an emergency generating station for the London Underground. On its riverside wall is an odd piece of narrative street art.

10 Continue past Trinity Hospital almshouses into Crane Street. The Trafalgar Tavern on the corner was famous in the 1800s for its whitebait dinners. Follow the river path past the Trafalgar, and by the Visitor Centre turn left into King William Walk, with the Cutty Sark on your right. Go right into College Approach and cross at the pedestrian crossing to continue right, to the entrance of Greenwich Market. Once a general market, it is now, at the weekend, an Aladdin's Cave, full of craft and food stalls.

11 Go through the market to the pub on the right-hand corner, where you turn right along Turnpin Lane into Greenwich Church Street. Here a right turn takes you to a double set of traffic lights leading back to your start point.

images